CHICAGO STUDIES IN THE HISTORY OF AMERICAN RELIGION

Editors

JERALD C. BRAUER
AND MARTIN E. MARTY

A CARLSON PUBLISHING SERIES

For a complete listing of the titles in this series,
please see the back of this book.

In the South the Baptists are the Center of Gravity

SOUTHERN BAPTISTS AND SOCIAL CHANGE, 1930-1980

Edward L. Queen II

PREFACE BY MARTIN E. MARTY

CARLSON
Publishing Inc

BROOKLYN, NEW YORK, 1991

Please see the end of this volume for a listing of all the titles in the Carlson Publishing Series *Chicago Studies in the History of American Religion*, edited by Jerald C. Brauer and Martin E. Marty, of which this is Volume 17.

Library of Congress Cataloging-in-Publication Data

Queen, Edward L.
   In the South the Baptists are the center of gravity : Southern
Baptists and social change, 1930-1980 / Edward L. Queen II.
      p.   cm. — (Chicago studies in the history of American
religion ; 17)
   Revision of thesis (Ph. D.)—University of Chicago, 1987.
   Includes bibliographical references and index.
   ISBN 0-926019-53-8 (alk. paper)
   1. Southern Baptist Convention—History—20th century.
2. Baptists—United States—History—20th century. 3. Church
controversies—Baptists. 4. Southern States—Religion. I. Title.
II. Series.
BX6462.3.Q44   1991
286'.132'0904—dc20   91-28027

Typographic design: Julian Waters

Typeface: Bitstream ITC Galliard

Case design: Alison Lew

Index prepared by Jonathan M. Butler.

Printed on acid-free, 250-year-life paper.

Manufactured in the United States of America.

Contents

An Introduction
to the Series

The *Chicago Studies in the History of American Religion* is a series of books that deal with topics ranging from the time of Jonathan Edwards to the 1970s. Three or four deal with colonial topics and three or four treat the very recent past. About half of them focus on the decades just before and after 1900. One deals with blacks; two concentrate on women. Revivalists, fundamentalists, theologians, life in the suburbs and life in heaven and hell, the Beecher family of old and a monk of new times, Catholics adapting to America and Protestants fighting one another—all these subjects assure that the series has scope. People of every kind of taste and curiosity about American religion will find some books to suit them. Does anything serve to characterize the series as a whole? What does the stamp of "Chicago studies" mean?

Yale historian Sydney Ahlstrom in *A Religious History of the American People*, as influential as any twentieth-century work in its field, pays respect to the "Chicago School" of American religious historians. William Warren Sweet, the pioneer in such studies (beginning in 1927) at Chicago and, in many ways, in America at large represented the culmination of "the Protestant synthesis" in this field. Ahlstrom went on to name two later generations of Chicagoans, including the seminal Sidney E. Mead and major figures like Robert T. Handy and Winthrop Hudson and ending with the two editors of this series. He saw them as often "openly rebellious" in respect to Sweet and his synthesis.

If, as Ahlstrom says, "a disproportionate number" of historians have some connection with the Chicago School, it must be said that the new generation represented in these twenty-one books carries on both the lineage of Sweet and something of the "openly rebellious" character that scholars at Chicago are encouraged to pursue. This means, for one thing, that the "Protestant synthesis" does not characterize their work. These historians question the canon of historical writing produced in the Protestant era even as many of them continue to pursue themes shaped in a Protestant culture. Few of them concentrate on the old "frontier thesis" that marked the early years of the school. The shift for most has been toward the urban and pluralist scene. They call into question, not in devastating rage but in steady patterns of inquiry, the received wisdom about who matters, and why, in American religion.

So it is that this series of books focuses on blacks, women, dispensationalists, suburbanites, members of "marginal" denominations, "ethnics" and immigrants as readily as it does on white men of progressive urban bent in mainstream denominations and of long standing in America. The authors relish religious diversity and enjoy discovering the power of people once considered weak, the centrality to the American plot of those once regarded as peripheral, and the potency of losers who were once disdained by winners. Thus this series enhances an understanding of an America overlooked by the people of Sweet's era two-thirds of a century ago when it all, or most of it, began.

Rebellion for its own sake would not long hold interest; it might tell more about the psychology of rebels and revisers than about their subject matter. Revision, better than rebellion, characterizes the scholars. Re+vision: that's it. There was an original vision that characterized the Chicago School. This was the contention that in secular America and its universities religion mattered, as a theme in the national past and as a presence in the present. Second, it argued that the study of religious history belonged not only in the seminaries and archives of denominations, but also in the rough-and-tumble of the secular university, where no religious meanings were privileged and where each historian had to make a case for the value of his or her story.

Other assumptions from the earliest days pervade the books in this series. They are uncommonly alert to the environment in which expressions of faith occur. That is, they do not take for granted that religion comes protected in self-evidently important and hermetically sealed packages. Churches and denominations are porous, even when they would be sealed off; they cannot be understood apart from the ways the social environs effect them, but their power to effect change in the environment demands equal and truly unapologetic treatment. These writers do not shuffle and mumble and make excuses for their existence or for the choice of apparently arcane subject matter. They try to present their narrative in such ways that they compel attention.

A fourth characteristic that colors these works is a refusal in most cases to be typed in a fashionable slot labeled, variously, "intellectual" or "institutional" history, "cultural" or "social" history, or whatever. While those which concentrate on magisterial thinkers such as Jonathan Edwards are necessarily busy with and devoted to his intellectual achievement, most of the books deal with figures who cannot be understood only as exemplars in a sequence of studies of "the life of the mind." Instead, their biographies and circumstances come very much into play. On the other hand, none of these writers is a reductionist who sees religion as "nothing but" this or that—"nothing but" the working out of believers' Oedipal urges or expressing the economic and class interests of the subjects. Social history becomes in its way intellectual history, even if the intellects are focused on something other than the theologians in the traditions might like to see.

Some years ago *Look* magazine interviewed leaders in various denominations. One was asked if his fellow believers considered that theirs was the only true faith. Yes, he said, but they did not believe that they were the only ones who held it. The editors of this series of studies and the contributors to it do not believe that the "Chicago School," whenever and whatever it was, is the only true approach to American religious history. And, if they did, they would not hold that Chicagoans alone held it. To do so would imply a strange solipsistic or narcissistic impulse that would be the death of collegiality in the historical field. They have welcomed the chance to be in a climate where their inquiries are given such encouragement, where they find a company of fellow scholars in the Divinity School, the History Department, and the Committee on the History of Culture, whence these studies first emerged, and elsewhere in a university that provides a congenial home for massed and massive concentration of a special sort on American religious history.

While the undersigned have been consistently involved, most often together, in all twenty-one books, we want to single out a third person mentioned in so many acknowledgment sections, historian Arthur Mann. He has been a partner in two or three dozen religious history dissertation projects through the years and has been an influential and decisive contributor to the results. We stand in his debt.

Jerald C. Brauer
Martin E. Marty

Editor's Preface

This book is an effort, a successful one, at unearthing and exposing to view a history and a process of change that is often overlooked by historians and citizens, but that can illumine much of what else they do. Edward L. Queen II shows how and why the South has been the poor relation, the snubbed relative, the embarrassment to be ignored by most American religious historians. Unless they were southerners, and the numbers of such in the company of histories of American religion until recently was small, they hurried elsewhere to pursue their preoccupations. They inherited a tradition of curiosity about what was called "the brain-working element in the North" and contented themselves with satisfying part of that curiosity.

New England always came off best, followed by the Episcopalian South and the Presbyterian middle colonies. Those who carried their interests into the nineteenth century followed northern Methodist, Baptist, and Disciples of Christ preachers to the frontier. Catholics, Lutherans, and Reformed immigrants from Ireland and the Continent came next into the scope of historians, while Jews, Mormons, and Christian Scientists were next in line.

The South, the place of slaveholders, strange people, losers, and victims, received negative notice when it drew notice at all. More's the pity for those who would understand American religion, the South, and contemporary social change, argues Queen, using historical narrative as his mode of conducting the argument. Fortunately, he does not adopt and hold to a defensive tone that would skew the story. He simply sets forth reasons to overcome neglect of the South and then through narrative gives ample reason for us to read.

The way to make a case, it becomes clear, is not to argue generalities but to point to specifics. The specific subject to which Queen points is hard to miss. The Southern Baptist Convention has become by far the largest Protestant denomination and, from the viewpoint of growth in size and influence, the only successful one among the large churches. It ministered to the poor southerners for a century and was then ready for Sunbelt prosperity as well as for expansion into the North even as it sent missionaries into the world.

Expansion has always been one of the themes that has held the group together. Theoretically a highly congregational body, it coheres, as Queen shows, because it is capable of drawing fierce loyalty and because it convinces its members that they should convert others.

Beyond that, its members fight. Once upon a time they fought the devil, the world, the flesh; they targeted the northern liberal denominations, the rival Methodists, the threatening Catholics. Some of these remain the enemy in the rhetoric of leftover fireaters, but nowadays Southern Baptists mainly fight Southern Baptists, over power and doctrine and positions having to do with the social and political order.

Queen goes sufficiently into the history of the convention before 1930 to set the stage for change in the subsequent half-century. He patiently exposes to view the presuppositions of its various parties. Few scholars that I have come across do more to help create an aura of plausibility about warring Baptist positions that have alienated others but have become life-and-death issues for them. This is as good a place as any to inform those who wish to know what Baptists contend for against other Baptists, and why. Insofar as nonpartisanship is possible on the part of bystanders, this is a nonpartisan document, but that does not mean that Queen writes with a dispassion that would fail the subject. He has been at home in the archives long enough to come back with the sources we need to make sense of things, and demonstrates the maturity that helps in that sense-making.

Nonreligious and nonsouthern Americans should read the book even in self-defense, but they will soon find positive reasons for doing so.

Martin E. Marty

Preface

Looking back through this work, completed three years ago, my first response is resignation. The resignation is brought on by the realization that it does not meet all my goals. It is made deeper by the realization that it never could do so.

When I began this work my goals were threefold. The first was to show from the documents of the period what Southern Baptists had said about the events of the time. I wanted to determine how they responded through the Depression, the Cold War, and the civil cights movement. This was important, given the predominance of the Southern Baptist Convention in the South. In doing this I discovered that these people said many different things. It was this complexity that I desired to convey in this work.

To relate their views to their socialization was the second goal. I wanted to correlate their views on events between 1930 and 1950 to their sources. The assumption behind this desire was that Southern Baptists had been enculturated into several value systems. Thus it was necessary to lay out these competing value systems and their sources. This act constitutes the first half of the work. I quickly discovered that these several value systems occasionally had shared elements, and often they were in conflict. When such conflict occurred I wanted to understand how members of the Southern Baptist Convention decided between the value systems. I then tried to interpret those decisions to discern why one value system dominated over another.

Finally I desired to illustrate how the events between 1930 and 1980, especially those from 1954 on, go far toward explaining the shift in the convention's mood from roughly 1976 on. I wanted to suggest some reasons why the Fundamentalists re-emerged after fifty years of relative quiescence and why they were relatively successful.

Any of these goals would have been sufficient to fill a book twice this size. But the fusion of the three and their relationship to one another made it seem reasonable to deal with them together. I leave it to the readers to determine how well it succeeds.

Acknowledgments

Upon finishing a lengthy work and sitting down to write the acknowledgments one is tempted to approach them the way one movie character (I think it was Jimmy Stewart in *Shenandoah*) approached the dinner blessing. The character, noting that he and his family had planted the crop, tended it, harvested it, and prepared it, concluded with "but we're going to thank you anyway, Lord." It takes only a short period of time, however, before one realizes that the debts owed far exceed the effort one personally expended. It is in the latter spirit that I offer these acknowledgments.

First I would like to recognize everything that I owe to my adviser Martin E. Marty, whose interest and knowledge permeate every page of this work. He has become more than a teacher and colleague. I would like to thank Jerald E. Brauer for his insightful and incisive comments. His ability to grasp the heart of the issues and to readily ascertain the weaknesses of the work have kept me from many errors. David Tracy has been the source of much encouragement throughout the past several years, not only in this project but in others. His optimism, his faith, and his friendship have been a source of strength and of help.

It is also incumbent upon me to thank the staff of the Baptist Historical Library and Archives and the E. C. Dargan Research Library of the Sunday School Board of the Southern Baptist Convention. Bill Sumners, the archivist, Pat Brown, the librarian, along with the entire staff were most helpful and friendly during the course of my several research trips.

Without the love and concern of friends like David White, David and Laura Gruber (whose willingness to allow me to reside with them while in Nashville made this work possible), DeAne Lagerquist, and Octavia Fallwell, none of this could have happened. Bruce Grelle, Chris Hinze, and Barry Stenger did more than their share by listening to complaints, reading chapters, and offering advice.

To my parents for their love, encouragement, and concern, as well as their constant belief in me. This is as much their achievement as mine. And finally to Hallie, because.

In the South the Baptists are the Center of Gravity

Introduction

The study of social change or, more precisely for this study, people's responses to social change, is exceedingly complex. It attempts to explain not only how, but why, people and groups respond to alterations in the conditions surrounding them. Analysis of change is equally difficult, for it attempts to discuss a continuous process with a static and event-oriented language. To understand change itself is a intricate endeavor. There are wide differences between short-term and long-term change. A drought lasting three months engenders different responses from one lasting three years. Change is reciprocal. Not only does it alter those to whom it happens (everyone to some extent), but individuals in responding to change structure and order it in ways related to what they had known previously.

Change does not occur like some magic trick. There is no abracadabra after which everything is different. Elements of the same society experience change at different rates. It is not too extreme to suggest that many of the problems involving social change result from a time lag between an event and its internalization, or a discovery and its explanation. Regardless of the magnitude of change, the past still remains. In fact, more of what was old continues than what is newly made. Whether the changes are in the realm of knowledge, government, or technology, large segments of the prechange world remain. Some of these remnants are vestigial like the linguistic continuance of the phrases "rising" and "setting" sun, others are far more active in our lives and in directing the way we think.

Analysis of responses to change presents larger problems than change itself. In studying responses to change one attempts to state how people, both individually and collectively, respond to events. Yet people, even in the same society, respond at different rates and in different ways. This is especially true in larger, more complicated societies where the options are greater and the penalties for deviance appear weaker. As a result, students of change tend to find themselves in the position of making general statements about a society despite the fact that such statements cannot hold.

The year 1980, the closing date for this study, found both the American South and the Southern Baptist Convention (SBC) in the middle of many internal conflicts and struggles. Both were in periods of change, but these were the beginnings of new struggles and new changes resulting from the complex forces and events that had affected both of them since 1930. It is important to remember that moments of change are the results of previous transformations. Change demands new responses, creates new conflicts. In this project I illuminate how Southern Baptists responded to and dealt with the alterations in the world between 1930 and 1980.

This is important because both the Southern United States and the Southern Baptist Convention have been treated as poor relations in the study of United States history. The South and Southerners have suffered under the ignominy of second-class citizenship since the Civil War. Treatments of the South's history illuminate the claim made by Theodor Adorno and Max Horkheimer that under Enlightenment tied to the dominant mode of production, to be a victim is to deserve to be a victim. "It is most pleasurable to inflict humiliation where misfortune has already hit hard. The less danger there is for those above, the more pleasure they will derive from the anguish they are about to inflict."[1] While there are several exceptions to this, the dominant mode of writing and thinking about the American South has been to assume that it was evil. As one writer has put it, "Being a white Southerner is a lot like being Eichmann's daughter: People don't assume you're guilty, but they wonder how you've been affected."[2] The progressive historian William Appleman Williams noted that "the visceral essay on the white Southerner as second-class citizen has yet to be written. C. Vann Woodward is just too damn polite. And Norman Mailer has not considered it important enough."[3]

Southern religion has suffered even more. When not ignored it has been vilified. It is unfortunate that the one person to have been most interested in writing about Southern religion has been its most vitriolic despiser, H. L. Mencken. His columns on the South and his reporting on the Scopes trial generally provide the background for understanding (?) Southern religion. The South has served as the whipping boy for the United States and Southern religion as the source for its failings. But the South and Southerners have not been the only sources of evil in the world, or even in this country. As Maury Maverick, the New Deal representative from Texas, pointed out, Sacco and Vanzetti were not hanged in Alabama, and Tom Moody was not imprisoned in Tennessee. Today one might add that Soledad is not in South Carolina.[4]

This is not to imply that the South did not suffer from many failures and even evils. It is only to suggest that the history of the South has been more complicated than those failures. If the South has been the bastion of conservatives and the backward looking, one might ask why so much of the progressive legislation of both the Woodrow Wilson and Franklin Roosevelt eras bear the names of Southern representatives and senators. To write about the South means that one has to rewrite about the South. The prejudices and assumptions of popular and journalistic writing must be ignored, both the unthinking negatives and the romantic legends.

Religion in the South, however, has not engaged the mind of most of its academic historians. This is true even of its better chroniclers. This is a confusing set of affairs since most of the latter have recognized the importance of Southern religion on its people and its region. When one talks about Southern religion to a great extent one talks about Baptists—Southern Baptists, black Baptists, primitive Baptists, two-seed-in-the-spirit Baptists. Just counting the Southern Baptist Convention and the major black Baptist conventions gives one a minimum of 35 to 40 percent of the population of the South. The impact of Baptists on the South, and particularly the Southern Baptist Convention on white Southerners, is great if for no other reason than their numbers. Despite this, however, few have bothered to examine in detail the attitudes of the SBC and its membership within their own terms. Far too often what little work that has been done has looked at Southern history and seen what the SBC has done or, as is generally the case, failed to do and dismissed it as a cultural religion and as an apologist for the evils in Southern society. Why, however, cannot the denomination be studied within its own terms? If anthropologists and sociologists with their fictitious value-free social scientific analysis can make such occurrences as suttee understandable, why not the actions and belief systems of the South and Southerners?

This book examines the responses of the members of the Southern Baptist Convention to events that transpired between 1930 and 1980. The premise ✓ is that the actions of the Southern Baptist Convention—the largest (white) denomination in the South—and its members might tell us a great deal about the period and the struggles involved. The internal conflicts of the SBC might be reflective of the internal conflicts of the Southern states and even the United States as a whole. To study the convention on its own terms might even be illustrative of why it could not lead its members on certain issues, but could on others. It might tell us why it was relatively quiet on civil rights issues, but not as quiet as some have assumed, and outspoken on issues of religious freedom.

Another focus is the fact that institutions always are immersed in a culture and a society. They reflect the limits as well as the hopes of their society. Religious institutions are bound by space and time, yet they claim to be transcendental. As instruments of the divine they transcend human and temporal limitations. As human creations, however, they do this only partially. Religions constantly operate under tension. They are bound and limited by their humanity, including their use of human language, yet they attempt to speak to the unlimited and unbounded power of the divine. To dismiss a religion as reflecting its culture is absurd; to assume it does not reflect its culture is equally so. It is just as absurd, if not blasphemous, to assume that because a religion reflects space/time limitations it does not aspire to reflect the divine.

Finally I assume that responses to change must be made. These responses are not always conscious, and they do not always mean acceptance of the changes. To choose to resist change is to recognize that it is occurring, or has occurred. Change, like history of which it is a part, takes place behind our backs to a large extent. While irrevocably linked with human actions, it is not equally linked to the actions of all. With all actions there are unintended results, and those results are the part that can be said to take place behind our backs. When talking about change it is important to avoid language that gives it the aura of inevitability. While change in general is inevitable, particular changes are not. Inevitability is the language given to past events by present interpreters. For history and historians the awareness that things could have been different is important. This awareness gives tragedy its pathos and humanity its hope. It is this hope, which assumes a future, that makes history possible.

The purposes of this project are themselves varied, ranging from the exceedingly simple to the somewhat convoluted. At the most immediate level this book determines how Southern Baptists responded to the events from the Depression through the election of Ronald Reagan as president. It studies the responses of a group over time, to see what they said and did through electrification, integration, atomic warfare, and the new morality. It takes seriously the concept of the *longue durée*. In this fifty-year period one could experience many different events and people. An adult in 1930 could have grown up knowing Confederate veterans and could have died after seeing men walk on the moon. The importance of long periods of time is best summed up in a half-humorous phrase of Willie Morris. In talking about how much of the South had become integrated he remarked, correctly, that the churches will be the last to go and only the undertaker will take care of that.[5] History and change, while depending so much on the new, also depend on death, an experience covered only over time.

This book also illuminates the complexities within the Southern Baptist Convention. These complexities owe their existence to many sources, not the least of which is that there are several Souths. There exists the South of the Atlantic coast of North and South Carolina, Virginia, and eastern Georgia. There is the South of the hills and mountains consisting of the western parts of the Carolinas and Virginia, north Georgia and Alabama, eastern Tennessee and Kentucky, and northern Arkansas. There is the Deep South of Georgia, Alabama, Mississippi, Louisiana, and northern Florida. There is the Southwest of Texas and Oklahoma. While these regions share many commonalities, they also are very different. These differences are reflected in their responses to issues and events.

The plurality in the SBC is not due only to intraregional differences but to the complexity of its membership as well. The denomination contains sharecroppers and governors, bank presidents and union organizers. These members all have opinions and views that conflict and converge. The SBC always has been composed of a myriad of voices, and this cacophony of tones needs to be heard.[6]

Traditionally two shared interests have prevented this cacophony from becoming a babel. These were a commitment to the denomination itself and to world evangelism. As a result of certain changes between 1930 and 1980, this consensus began to break down during the 1970s. While few Southern Baptists questioned the latter commitment, differences regarding its meaning increased. The former, however, began to collapse. With the increasing polarization of politics not only in the United States but throughout the world, consensus, upon which the SBC depended mightily, became increasingly unimportant. Single-issue politics, the expansion of communication technology, mobility, and social dislocation created a series of realities that weakened the commitments and attachments of many. Attachment to the denomination itself was one of these victims. The Fundamentalists' attempt in the 1970s and 1980s to dominate and control the denomination was linked to their view of it only as a tool to further their work. In their minds, people disagreeing with them only weakened the functioning of the tool. They failed to see that the denomination itself had meaning and value to many people, and always included differences of opinion and theology.[7]

The plurality that enabled a Brooks Hays and a W. A. Criswell, an Adrian Rogers and an E. Y. Mullins to be elected presidents of the convention is being challenged by those who feel that the convention should be only one thing and one way. This new struggle owes its existence to what has transpired during the past half century. What this was and what it has meant are the fundamental questions to which this book suggests some answers.

Finally, to write is to express the hope that a reader might learn something and find guidance for actions. That indeed is the ultimate purpose of this book. By suggesting how the Southern Baptist Convention got to where it is today, the hope is that some may take those hows and whys and use them to create a better future.

ONE

The Southern Baptist Convention

The Southern Baptist Convention, despite its size—at fifteen million members the largest Protestant denomination in the country—is relatively unknown (outside of the South) and unstudied.[1] In the Southern states the Southern Baptist Convention dominates the religious landscape, constituting a plurality of all church members. The percentage of Southern Baptists in the individual states ranges from a low of 27.7 in Louisiana to a high of 64.1 in Alabama.[2] As the dominant religious body it exerts tremendous moral authority in that region, and to a great extent has created the moral ethos of the South. In one sense Southern Baptists have assisted in creating the Southern value system. This is especially true in the areas of personal morality—attitudes toward beverage alcohol, gambling, sexuality, etc.[3] This is not to imply that conflicting value systems are nonexistent, but that to a great extent they are defined in terms of their difference from that ethos.

Religiously this Southern Baptist predominance has an impact on other denominations in the South. This is true not only of those Protestant denominations one might expect to show similarities in religious behavior, but also of disparate bodies including the Episcopal, Roman Catholic, and Jewish. All of these are marked by a higher rate of religious activity than their counterparts in the North, and the two former are much less liturgical. All tend to share in the moral ethos of the region. As Samuel Hill has noted, "In the south Baptist and Methodist churches are landmarks and other denominations vary from their historical practice in order to fit into the religious pattern of those two denominations."[4]

Despite its size and influence, the Southern Baptist Convention remains a relatively unstudied denomination. As with all denominations there have been the requisite number of filiopietistic histories, in-house attempts at documenting denominational birth, growth, and expansion.[5] Yet there has been no in-depth and analytical study of the SBC over time. This is surprising given its size and its dominance in such a large region of the country. This absence of study is compounded by an ignorance of the denomination. Since it is common for many different organizations and many individual congregations to share the name Baptist without belonging to the Southern Baptist Convention, there exists a tendency to lump all Baptists together. This becomes a special problem given the strong regional identification of the Southern Baptist Convention with the Southern United States. The ignorance of the SBC combines with a general ignorance of, and prejudice toward, the South to produce a most negative image. Mention the term Baptist and the name Jerry Falwell arises immediately. Yes, he is a Baptist from the South—Lynchburg, Virginia—but he is not a Southern Baptist. While some Baptists are members of the Jerry Falwell-led Moral Majority, the convention itself takes no position regarding the Falwell harangues, just as it is neither a member of the National Association of Evangelicals nor of the National Council of Churches.

The Southern Baptist Convention is, to a great extent, a body sui generis. Historically it has attempted to avoid creedal statements to concentrate on the work of evangelization. It grants the designation "church" only to the local congregation—hence the term Southern Baptist Convention.[6] It rejects centralized authority yet has the massive bureaucracy needed to run an organization with fifteen million members, 34,610 churches, 4,000 missionaries, and a budget of $90 million.[7] Its democracy has been likened to a log raft. "You cannot guide the thing very well; you wallow all over the place; and your feet are always wet—but you can never sink a log raft. If you keep trying you eventually get to a destination."[8]

This democracy, which has been a major strength of the denomination, is also a stumbling block, hindering the denomination's ability to take a leadership role in responding to changes in its society. While democracy kept it "responsive to the common people, it also enslaved their churches and institution to the prejudices of the people."[9] To a great extent all institutions are enslaved by their members; to those whom even the most authoritarian institutions address their claims for legitimacy and who in a noncoercive situation may simply ignore the pronouncements of the most hierarchical of bodies, e.g., American Catholics and the Magisterium's pronouncements on birth control. As a democratic institution dependent on its members for funds and for direction, there has been a concerted effort in the Southern Baptist Convention to deemphasize those issues whose disruptive nature could have divided it. For Southern Baptists it was imperative that nothing impede their primary mission, the bringing of the world to Christ. Democracy within the convention, therefore, always tilted it toward accepting the values and beliefs of the members and their society.

At this point one should notice that three issues could act to mitigate an active involvement by the SBC in attempts to transform society: the institutional structure of the denomination, its democratic nature, and its unwillingness to endanger its evangelical mission. The first of these makes it impossible for the institution to direct the activities of the individual congregations or members. The convention itself lacks any authority beyond that of moral suasion.

Second, its democracy prevents it from going against the majority of its members on any issue. This also involves the element of authority, specifically the convention's lack of authorization to speak for all of its members. This means that messengers—they are not delegates because the authority of the local church cannot be delegated—represent their society and their fellow church members in such a way that they see no reason to challenge fundamentally their society and its value system. Even if the possibility occurred to them they would be unable to implement any changes, beyond structural ones. There also exists the threat of the membership's use of the power of the purse to prevent the implementation of policies they dislike.

Finally, theological differences have been glossed over by vague affirmations of faith in attempts to include everyone and avoid conflicts. This is not to imply that there are no conflicts, only that conflict is not allowed to move beyond a certain point. All conflicts end where the "Great Commission" begins. What Wayne Flynt has said about Southern Evangelicals in general is especially true of the Southern Baptist Convention.

> The unity on the central religious issue is the force which held urban and rural, conservative, moderate, and liberal evangelicals together. They could slay each other with Biblical quotations, on race, evolution, the millennium and women deacons, then reunite on behalf of world evangelical outreach.[10]

Walter Shurden has made this even more explicit. "The SBC cemented the new denomination, not around doctrinal uniformity, but by 'organizing' a plan for eliciting, combining and directing the energies of the whole denomination in one sacred effort, for the propagation of the gospel."[11]

Southern Baptists see themselves as acting primarily on the spiritual level. This is where they have their authority. The church exists in obedience to

Jesus Christ, who is its Lord, "and has no mission on the earth save the carrying out of his will. It must not to form alliances of any kind with the state so that it surrenders any of its own functions or assumes any functions of civil government."[12] It takes seriously Jesus' injunction that one should render those things unto Caesar that are Caesar's, and unto God those that are God's. This spiritual level is also a level on which the state has no authority, and from the earliest period of their history Baptists have been in the forefront of the struggles for religious liberty. However, unlike other religious groups with similar positions, Baptists never rejected the authority of the magistracy to uphold the civil order. In fact this issue prevented a union between the early English Baptists and the Waterlander Mennonites.[13]

While Baptists felt that was wrong for the state to attempt to run the church, they also felt that the church should not attempt to run the state. For the most part the convention's political activity has consisted of efforts to maintain the disestablishment and free exercise clauses of the First Amendment. Certainly while church members in their position as private citizens have the right, even the obligation, to work for godly and moral governmental policies, that is not the position, or duty, of the church.

> Other denominations make it a part of their program to move into the area of politics, social problems, and other secular areas, but Southern Baptists throughout the years have sought to stay clear of political situations, however, they do preach and stand for their members acting Christian in all of the relationships of life. All of us as Christian citizens are expected to conduct ourselves in the spirit of Christ.[14]

In order to understand the impact that being a Southern Baptist had upon its membership, a detailed look at Southern Baptist history and doctrines is necessary. But first certain assumptions must be made explicit. In this period I am examining how one group of people—the Southern Baptists—in a particular region—the Southern United States—dealt with social, political, and economic change in a given period—1930-1980. Like everyone, these people had experienced, and continued to experience, the processes of socialization. One must remember, however, that human beings are not socialized into one group only. Socialization occurs from many sources, some of which have competing and contradictory value systems.

For Southern Baptists one of those groups was the denomination itself. Through being raised within a church home, or by entering into church fellowship later in life, one encounters, becomes a part of, the Southern

Baptist version of the Christian life. The denomination, therefore, does not simply mirror the attitudes of white Southerners; it assists in the creation of the values and attitudes of a large segment of that population. The value and belief system of the Southern Baptist life becomes a part of the individual. This affects one alongside those systems of socialization determined by class, professional, educational, and other groupings to which one belongs.

For most Southern Baptists another major source of socialization was their identity as white Southerners. Quite often there was conflict between the value systems of Southerner and Baptist. The demands put on individuals as members of both groups resulted in a series of individual and group conflicts from 1930 to 1980. Because these two groupings are so important to an understanding of these people, the history and idea systems of both must be brought out in detail.

The Southern Baptist Convention entered the world on May 8, 1845. At that time Baptists had been in the South for nearly 150 years. The early Baptists had made a nuisance of themselves throughout the colonies, especially in Virginia and Massachusetts Bay where they came into conflict with the religious establishments. In response they were harried out of those areas at the end of whips and cudgels. Even after the advent of laws of religious tolerance, relationships between Baptists and the authorities were strained. Baptist principles were such that they rejected not only the state's claim to establish a particular religion, but also attempts to levy taxes in support of any all religious bodies, including their own. Most Baptists rejected attempts by the authorities to license or control the activities of ministers as well.

This ongoing conflict between Baptists and the politico-religious establishments in the various colonies led them to be among those Southern colonists most supportive of the revolutionary cause. While loyalties in the American Revolution owed much to class and regional differences, religion was not the least important. This is illustrated by the active role taken by Baptists to achieve complete religious disestablishment in Virginia and in securing a Bill of Rights to the United States Constitution.[15]

Baptists in the South experienced phenomenal growth from 1789 to 1845. Like Methodists, Presbyterians, and Congregationalists, Baptists were well suited to evangelizing the American frontier. While many have been inclined to attribute these successes to vague psychological terms like "individualism," "frontier mentality," and "emotionalism," there were factors of a more substantive nature at work. The institutional structures of the Methodist and Presbyterian churches assisted them in their attempts at domestic missions.

11

This especially was true for the Methodists, who through their system of circuit riders could cover wide areas with relatively few men. But the institutional structures also slowed these groups. The need for a candidate to be licensed by a presbytery or an association, and the educational requirements, hindered the ability of Presbyterians and Congregationalists to enter the field. Similar, though weaker, constraints operated on the Methodists.

Such constraints, however, were unknown to Baptist ministers. Since the spirit of God bloweth where it will and since the local church controlled the ordination of ministers, formal education, ministerial examinations, and centralized bodies were not necessary for the creation of Baptist ministers. The only criteria were a conversion experience and a call from God to preach the gospel. This resulted in the existence of a larger pool from which Baptists could draw their candidates for the ministry. Baptists in a remote community could start a new church without waiting for the arrival of a minister from outside. Quite often the Baptist church was the only one in the area, although it was closely followed by the Methodist circuit rider. As such it attracted residents of the community who had been of a different communion prior to their westward movement. While some certainly must have returned to their original fold when the leadership caught up with its membership, others undoubtedly remained Baptists and added to the denomination's growth.

The number of these "converts" was surpassed by the real converts, those who had no previous religious affiliation—a much larger group in 1800 than today. The Baptists were there and ready to provide church services. They also provided those elements of human associationalism attendant upon religious membership. Religion provided the community and sociability lacking on the frontier.

As institutions, churches provided a level of social order and structure. Such needs were not linked solely to the frontier. The immigrant churches served a similar function in cities during the late nineteenth and early twentieth centuries. The same was true in the upper Midwest and the Great Plains, where Lutheran and Catholic churches served the needs of the Scandinavian and German immigrants on a very different frontier. Synagogues and churches serve a similar function today when advice columnists recommend that singles and the widowed attend religious services to meet people and to find community. People on the frontier joined churches for the same reason people have always done so (at least since joining was an option)—for religious and social reasons. They quite often joined Baptist churches because they were available.

12

Another reason for the growth of Baptist churches was their class and social status. Baptist churches drew most of their membership from laboring folk in the South, both black and white. This is to say that they most readily attracted those people who formed the majority of the region's populace. There are numerous reasons for this. The first involved the conflicts in colonies like Virginia between the established church and the nonconforming bodies, especially the Baptists. As the established church, the Anglican church belonged to the elite of the region and had its strength along the Atlantic coast and those rivers forming the major transportation system of the Carolinas and Virginia. In these areas attempts were made to retain the English parish system. In the backcountry with its sparse population there was little money to support a paid clergyman, even if a candidate willing to settle in such an area could be found. The Church of England made little effort to reach the backcountry, and the efforts that were made dissipated quickly with the outbreak of the American Revolution. Baptists became identified with resistance to the English parish system, and the Regulator movement—an armed rebellion against the colonial authorities during the 1760s—had its greatest strength in the areas with the largest concentration of Baptists.[16]

During the eighteenth and nineteenth centuries most Baptist ministers worked at second jobs as either farmers or laborers. They shared the economic trials and struggles of their membership. For many, nonchurch work was their primary source of income. Under such a system even the poorest church could afford a minister, at least occasionally. Some ministers served several churches—preaching at each one on a regular basis. Such occurrences were known in Southern Baptist churches well into the twentieth century.[17]

Baptist churches grew because Baptist ministers were readily available. The organizational and administrative difficulties involved in supplying a minister were nonexistent. Combined with this was the fact that the economic consequences of paying a minister were not preeminent. If the minister made a living at another job he could be had regardless of the ability of the members to pay him. There were theological ramifications to this issue as well. Whereas there is the biblical admonition not to muzzle the ox that treads the threshing floor, there is also the biblical story of Simon Magus and the refusal of Peter and John to accept his money, claiming that the gifts of God were not for sale.[18] While not a major issue, the salary of the minister was a nagging one. There always remained the conflict between the peddling of the word of God and the right of the minister to a living wage. But did not Paul earn his living as a tentmaker?

Baptist churches along the frontier grew because the Baptists were there and because they welcomed every member on an equal basis. The importance of Baptist democracy must not be denigrated here. There existed to a greater extent than elsewhere in their world a functional equality in the Baptist churches, including, in some instances, an equality between master and slave.[19] Brooks Hays provided a most eloquent statement of this Baptist equality.

> My first Sunday School teacher was a blacksmith. Later I was instructed by a coal miner, whose gnarled hands symbolized for me the hardships of the period's life. . . .
>   The woman who did my mother's washing sat on the same pew with my parents. "Miss Helen," mother called her, for she had status too. . . . Her vote in church conference had the same weight as my mother's and father's, and her presence on that third pew with them remained for me an authentic symbol of Baptist democracy.[20]

However, as civilization caught up to the frontier, the early pioneers became comfortable settlers and fell under the watchful gaze of their neighbors. They became increasingly associated with the social system and its values. In the South this system included black chattel slavery. While most Baptists in the South, like most Southerners, did not own slaves, they became increasingly imbued with the values of slaveowning society and suspicious of attacks on it. The Southern Baptist Convention was founded due to conflicts over slavery.

In 1814 the Baptist churches in the United States formed the General Convention to supervise their mission work.[21] During the late 1830s and early 1840s there was increasing antislavery agitation within the convention, and despite its official neutrality many members of the Home Mission Society were active in abolition work. While Baptist leaders from both the South and North struggled to prevent the issue of slavery from intruding into their missionary efforts, it was brought to a head in 1844 by the Georgia Baptist Executive Committee. In that year they submitted the name of James E. Reeve to the Home Missionary Society for appointment as a missionary. They simultaneously volunteered the information that Mr. Reeve was a slaveholder. The Executive Committee of the Home Missionary Society refused to consider the application because it constituted a test and violated thereby the society's stance of neutrality over slavery and its resolution denying anyone the right to intrude the subject of slavery into the society. This state of affairs was exacerbated when the Alabama Baptist Convention meeting in November 1844 addressed a resolution to the General Convention demanding that it explicitly state that privileges were equally available to slaveholders and nonslaveholders. The General Convention responded in the negative, stating that if a slaveholder were to offer himself as a missionary "and should insist on retaining them as his property we could not appoint him. One thing is certain, we can never be a party to any arrangement which would imply approbation of slavery."[22] When this correspondence became public, Baptists in the South were incensed. In response the Virginia Foreign Mission Society issued a call for a meeting of the Baptists in the South, "to confer on the best means of promoting the Foreign Mission cause, and other interests of the Baptist denomination in the South."[23] The date was set for May 1845 and Augusta, Georgia, the place.

Like the Presbyterians and the Methodists, the split among the American Baptists was linked to the split in the nation. The reason for the split was slavery, but unlike the other two denominations Baptists never rejoined their Northern brethren. In fact, while the American Baptists—as the Northern Baptists came to be known—waned in number and became increasingly liberal, theologically the Southern Baptist Convention waxed exceedingly strong, growing in strength and favor with the Lord. While doing so they remained closely identified with the Southern states. This specific identification of the Southern Baptist Convention with the former Confederacy has had a tremendous impact on them both.

In 1877, thirty-two years after the founding of the Southern Baptist Convention, there were Southern Baptist churches in only fourteen states and the District of Columbia. These were the eleven states of the former Confederacy plus Kentucky, Maryland, and Oklahoma. By 1917, only three more states had been added—New Mexico, Illinois, and Missouri. While from 1917 to the present churches affiliated with the Southern Baptist Convention would come to be located in every state, the overwhelming majority of its membership remained in the South. Of the approximately fifteen million Southern Baptists, roughly 90 percent of them live in thirteen states, the eleven states of the Confederacy plus Oklahoma and Kentucky. They draw their strength and their beliefs from the South, just as the South is affected by the religious and moral forms of the Southern Baptists. This is not only because Southern Baptists were overwhelmingly Southern, but it was also a conscious claim that the relationship between the Southern states and the Southern Baptist Convention was more than an accident of history. There existed a feeling that the Baptists as a whole, especially the Southern Baptist Convention as a bastion against modernism and liberalism, and the South as

15

a region were ordained to play a special role in the bringing of America and the world to Christ.

Before the war there had been a tendency toward this type of thinking, but it greatly increased following it. After the Civil War the South had a fundamental theological problem unknown in the North. Why had the South lost? The glorious South whose men were braver, whose women more virtuous, and whose cause truer should not have lost. God would not have allowed it. Yet they had lost and God must have willed it. Why? Certainly not because their cause was wrong. No! It was because God had other plans for the Southern people and had to chastise them for their sins—like the Israelites of old—so they could better serve God's will. Does not God chastise and test those whom God loves? Certainly. The South, therefore, had to remain in the Union in order that its pure orthodox religion could be used as an antidote to the theological liberalism, modernism, and unbelief rampant in the North.

This was not merely a rhetorical device to be used as a spiritual sop to those who had experienced a devastating war and were left with nothing but destruction, defeat, and despair. It was a widely held belief in the Southern states well into the twentieth century. Following the First World War the primary importance of the South in Christianizing America and the world reappeared. When Southern Baptists surveyed the destruction of the old world in Europe, particularly of the German nation (the source of all modernisms), they saw their purpose at hand. The world needed to be rebuilt, a new order created, one in which the possibilities for Southern Baptists were infinite. It was the South's time to act. Southern Baptists "never before confronted such tremendous opportunities. As goes America, so goes the world. Largely as goes the South, so goes America. And in the South is the Baptist center of gravity of the world."[24]

The idea of the South and Baptists as related remained a dominant theme. Southern Baptists did not only hold the most correct form of Christianity, but the South itself was a more virtuous region of the country, having been spared the vices of prosperity, urbanization, and modernism. While it seems odd to see prosperity listed as a vice, especially from a region as poverty-stricken as the South, it should not. This is not to say that wealth itself was considered an evil, but it was seen as a major deterrent to an uplifting spiritual life. "The most dangerous thing under the sun is prosperity. People do right more often under adversity than they do under prosperity. Very few people can stand success."[25] The biblical story of the rich young ruler provided a good illustration of this lesson. While one does not find a blanket condemnation of wealth, there are constant warnings regarding the perils associated with it. One can even find a recommendation of foreign aid based on the premise that it not only helps the less fortunate, but also strengthens the national moral fiber weakened by materialism.[26]

> Having more ready wealth, men and women are the more tempted to invest it in luxuries of questionable value. Without the influence of a real community and under the social pressure of the large and varied city population people are more easily led to live loosely.[27]

This tendency of prosperity is aggravated by the pressures of the city. For Southern Baptists, and Southerners in general, the mythology of the rural life as morally superior to urban life is strong. Cities are cold and immoral. The natural limiting systems of family and community break down in them. Because of this the temptations of the city are greater and one more likely to fall victim to them, especially drunkenness and lust. The South, a primarily rural area in 1930, became predominantly urban by 1980. This threatened the value system of many Southerners and Southern Baptists. There was no attempt to halt the process of urbanization but instead a call for a determined effort to evangelize the city.

Southern Baptists were not, however, merely a social group residing in a particular region. They were, and are, members of a religious institution with religious beliefs and values. To ignore this is to ignore their reality. Actions and behaviors of Southern Baptists were not conditioned solely by their social position and history. They lived out their religious beliefs.

Religion is, among other things, a spiritual phenomenon having to do with the divine, in claim if not in fact. Religious beliefs must be taken seriously as such, not dismissed casually or reduced to a series of responses to social and material factors. These beliefs are held by a large number of people and have an impact on them, their view of the world, and their responses to that world.

What, then, are Baptist beliefs? Many, if not most, are beliefs held by the majority of other Christians. They believe in an omnipotent God, the divinity of Jesus, who was born of a virgin, crucified and died, rose on the third day, sits at the right hand of the father, and will come again to judge the quick and the dead. Given Baptists' distaste for creedal formulations, however, it is rare that one would hear the above recited in a Baptist service. Baptists, therefore, are Christians, orthodox in their beliefs, nonliturgical, nonsacramental, and noncreedal. Their ecclesiology is generally low. These elements in this combination set them apart, and make them Baptists.[28]

Certainly many of the beliefs discussed below are shared with other religious groups, but none combines them in the same way as do Baptists. Finally it also necessary to interject a caveat. When discussing Baptist beliefs on any but the most general level several problems arise. The first is that the historical Baptist doctrine of soul competency or freedom absolves any Baptist from holding any particular formulation of faith, hence the distaste for creedal formulations, especially as statements of orthodoxy. This is as true for the more historic creeds and confessions—Nicene, Athanasian, Apostles'—as for others more recent—Augsburg, Westminster—and even for the dominant Baptist confessions—the New Hampshire Declaration and the Philadelphia Confession. With this fact in mind we can proceed.

There are several historic Baptist positions. Several are specifically theological, while others are more practical but with important theological implications both formulated and unformulated.

Baptists believe in the omnipotence of God and the divinity of Jesus, who as the Christ was crucified for the sins of all and resurrected on the third day. This act is sufficient for the salvation of all (John 3:16), if only they would accept it. God wills that all should be saved and come to a knowledge of the truth (1 Timothy 2:4). God does not force this on the wills of women and men but offers it freely and they may accept or reject it. God, however, does not simply fling the seeds of salvation out upon the fields with no preparation. God knows that our fallen species would always choose evil if left to itself. Still God cannot trample on the freedom, which He has imprinted on our souls. In order to respond to this situation God not only has sent Jesus as our mediator and redeemer, but also has provided the Gospel, the Holy Spirit, the church, the preacher, the sermon, and other means of persuading us to believe—first because God has chosen us, and second because we have chosen God.[29]

Those souls who have accepted freely the gift of salvation from God by undergoing a conversion experience in which they have been convicted of their sins, repented, and accepted their need for Jesus as their savior symbolize this new reality through the ordinance of baptism. Baptism is the immersion of the regenerate person in water in the name of the Father, the Son, and the Holy Spirit. Baptism symbolizes the remission of sins, fellowship with Christ in his death, burial, and resurrection, and a cleansing from all unrighteousness. Baptism does not bring these about. It simply signifies the regeneration in a person's heart previously accomplished through the workings of the Holy Spirit. For Baptists it is required for admission into church fellowship and for participation in the Lord's Supper.

The center of Baptist life is the individual congregation, the church. For Baptists the church is "a local body composed of believers in Jesus Christ who are associated together for the cultivation of the Christian life, the maintenance of the ordinances and discipline, and for the propagation of the Gospel."[30] The government of the church is democratic and autonomous. Every individual congregation is free and independent. It can be coerced neither by another congregation nor by any denominational body. It is a voluntary association of free individuals who in obedience to Christ have joined together in order to achieve purposes set forth by him. The church as an institution in obedience to God has no purpose on this earth other than the carrying out of the Lord's will. It is not to form alliances with the state that may require it to surrender any of its own functions or to assume any of the functions of civil government.[31]

This is the source of an important element of Baptist beliefs, the emphasis on the separation of church and state and religious freedom. Since their appearance in England in the early seventeenth century Baptists have been constantly exercised by the issue of religious freedom. Their rejection of religious establishment has caused them difficulties, from seventeenth-century England to twentieth-century Spain. In the United States they have been in the forefront in the continuous struggle to maintain Jefferson's wall of separation, though for reasons quite different from his.

As mentioned earlier, the activities of Baptist ministers in the American colonies greatly agitated the establishment. This led to a rather violent and ongoing conflict between the magistrates and the Baptist congregants. Whippings, imprisonment, and fines were not uncommon penalties for Baptist refusal to accept control by the civil government. Baptists came to their position as proponents of religious liberty via four main routes. The first was experiential. As an unestablished body in England and elsewhere Baptists often felt the knout of the religious establishments as wielded by the civil authorities. Unlike the Presbyterian and Congregational churches that preached tolerance when they were out of power and establishment when in power, Baptists never sought to form themselves as a religious establishment. In fact the one colony Baptists assisted in establishing, Rhode Island, was created as a haven for religious dissenters. The experience of persecution was not therefore sufficient to create a permanent commitment to religious liberty. Other sources in the Baptist belief system were equally necessary to provide them with the tools to build a relatively consistent and steadfast commitment.

The second source was the Baptist commitment to the individual's experience of faith through a free and voluntary act. Acceptance of Jesus as the Christ is a noncoercible reality for Baptists. Coercion produces, at best, an outward assent; it cannot produce an experiential trust and acceptance of God. The civil authorities may have the power to coerce actions, but not belief. However, once their attempts to coerce behavior intrudes upon the spiritual realm they become invalid, for we are called to trust in God rather than men. To coerce outward religious behavior through laws requiring church attendance, taxation, licensing of ministers is to violate the spiritual realm. It makes some hypocrites and others idolaters who place human laws and institutions above the laws of God.

The third and fourth of these sources must be considered together (in fact it is possible to understand one as emerging from the other as its logical derivation)—these are the priesthood of all believers and the liberty of conscience (soul freedom or competency). If the idea of the priesthood of all believers is taken seriously, then there can be no civil intermediary between God and the human person, just as there is no religious intermediary. If every person is her or his own priest, the idea of an established religion is absurd. The idea of such a privileged position is contradicted by the category itself.

This is especially true for those most interested in the spiritual realm. The problem of the worldly kingdom is basically unimportant, and until it is raised the issue remains fairly simple. The civil realm, at best, must limit itself to the realm of human mortal existence and leave the immortal conscience of the individual to God.[32]

Liberty of conscience flows readily from the two previous claims. If belief cannot be coerced and there exists no intermediary between the individual and God, the individual is completely and solely responsible before God regarding issues of conscience. This doctrine is not meant to imply that anything is right solely because someone holds it conscientiously. It means that given humanity's fallen nature, and that it sees through a glass darkly, the ability of every individual to pass religious judgment is equally distorted. The ability, therefore, to pass such a judgment resides solely with God. One may not, and cannot, pass the responsibility for one's conscience to another by claiming that one was coerced. The responsibility resides with the individual. Thomas Helwys stated this most succinctly in his response to the Divine Right claims of James I:

. . . our lord the King is but an earthly King, and he hath no aucthority as a King but in earthly causes, and if the Kings people be obedient and true subjects, obeying all humane lawes made by the King, our lord the King can require no more: for mens religion to God is betwixt God and themselves; the King shall not answer for it, neither may the King be judgd between God and man. Let them be heretikes, Turcks, Jewes or whatsoever, it apperteynes not to the earthly power to punish them in the least measure.[33]

Southern Baptists have a tradition of beliefs and activities that exert a strong and continuous impact on their decision-making and their behavior. Quite often Baptists remained consistent with this heritage, at other times contradictory forces exerted a stronger power over them. In this they are no different from others who find themselves pulled in opposite directions.

Although their understanding of themselves as Baptists provides members of the SBC with traditions affecting their behaviors, this has not been the only source operating on them. They also have a set of traditions as Southerners, and as Americans. Understanding the Baptist influences enables one to see Southern Baptists as a people with religious traditions and beliefs that structured their views of the world and provided the bases for their attempts to deal with the changes they experienced. Equally important are the sources and elements of Southern society and culture that created the world most Southern Baptists inhabited and that deeply affected their processes of socialization.

TWO

The American South: History and Change

Between 1930 and 1980 the Southern states participated in the great social upheavals experienced by the country as a whole. In order to grasp how Southern Baptists responded to change in this period it is necessary to describe what those changes were. Only by recognizing the magnitude of change can one grasp the extent of adaptation that took place. Whether these responses were considered and chosen, or the results of faits accompli, is irrelevant. Too often people have assayed to examine change in terms of rational choices, including choices to resist change, instead of looking at those changes to which people adapt slowly basically because that is the way things are. An example is responses to electrification. It was not the type of change that engendered a great deal of resistance, but it radically transformed society. Its impact is readily admitted, yet how individuals experiencing the process responded to it is rarely noted. One of the questions raised by such issues is, does a community's view of what is normative change when what *is* normative also changes? For example, as the South became increasingly urbanized did the normative picture of the typical Southern Baptist family, as portrayed in Baptist literature, shift its orientation from rural/farming toward a more urban orientation? If changes like these do occur, the next step is to examine how they do so, the resistance they meet, and how conflicts arising over them are resolved—if in fact they are.

While the changes undergone by the South were of the same type experienced by the nation as a whole, the magnitude was greater in the South. Even though the South narrowed the economic gap between it and the rest of the country, the lag remained. The South retained a distinctiveness in terms of the intensity of the change underwent and its relative poverty.

Change in the South also must be examined in light of the fact that so much of it was imposed from outside, or perceived as such. As John Shelton

Reed put it, "In a region which has had at least its share of the American experience of rapid social change, the one constant has been that nearly all of that change has been imposed from outside."[1] Individuals are related to their society and culture. Baptists in the South are Southerners, and most white Southerners belong to the Southern Baptist Convention. They are socialized into the values, norms, and perceptions of that society. Simultaneously they (re)create those norms and values. There exists an internal relation between people and their society. Modifications of a society must have an impact on its members, especially when those changes seem to challenge the bases of an individual's or group's self-definition. The situation in the South resulted in a unique set of realities to which Southerners had to respond.

√ The South has always been black and white. Since the 1600s, when the first blacks were brought to this country as indentured servants, a great deal of white energy has been expended on organizing and rationalizing the structures of this racial reality. The relationships of salvation to slavery, slavery to union, freedmen to politics, and segregation to law have agitated and dominated the thinking of white Southerners. The doctrine of white supremacy has been so strong that some observers have seen it as *the* central theme of Southern history. As Ulrich B. Phillips put it early in this century, the South "is and shall remain a white man's country."[2] Now that the civil rights movement has left an indelible mark on the South and the South still remains, the extremity of that statement has been proven false. But the truth behind it remains. To a great extent Southern history can be seen as a constant struggle of whites to live with and dominate blacks, and to rationalize that domination.

The second greatest event and determinant of Southern history owes its occurrence at least in part to the position of blacks. This is the Civil War and its aftermath. The South's defeat in this conflict still haunts it over one hundred years later. It constitutes a part of Southern distinctiveness as the only (white) segment of the American populace to have experienced defeat. As Lewis Killian puts it, in the South alone "school children are taught American history from the viewpoint of a nation that lost 'the War', a nation whose heroes were condemned as traitors and whose enemies were glorified in the rest of the country."[3] The *Harvard Encyclopedia of Ethnic Groups* put it this way:

> If the ancestors of most present-day Southerners had their way, there would be no question of whether they should be treated as an American ethnic group.

24

Southern whites remained . . . Americans against their will, a fact that has a great deal to do with their persistence as an identifiable group.[4]

Not only has that loss marked the South as different from the rest of the country, but the results of that loss served to create Southern distinctiveness as well. The mementoes of poverty and destruction lingered well into this century. While the North and West were alive with economic growth and progress, the states of the former Confederacy were attempting to rebuild a world whose infrastructure was nonexistent and whose social structure was in disarray. Not only the presence of an occupying army, but the tedious and unseemly business of stamping out democracy by destroying the Populist and Republican parties, as well as disfranchising most poor whites and all blacks delayed the reconstruction of an unreconstructed social order.

Another peculiarity of the South is the relative homogeneity of its population compared to the country as a whole.[5] This results primarily from the War and the South's black population. An example of this is that 80 percent of white Southerners belong to one of two religious denominations, Baptist or Methodist. In no other part of the country, with the exception of Utah, is there such religious homogeneity. The white population of the South is also more ethnically homogeneous than the rest of the country. The majority of the population traces its ancestry to the British Isles. This is a partial result of the dreadful poverty in the South during the period of greatest immigration, from 1865 to the 1920s. With the exception of the rare industrial city like Birmingham, there were no economic incentives to come to the South. Another factor was the difficulty in traveling to the region. The South's railway system lagged behind that of the Northeast and Midwest. The South lacked a major port of entry on the Atlantic Coast following the silting up of Charleston's Harbor in the late eighteenth century. Thus, the South did not attract other ethnic groups, as did the Northeast and Midwest.

The pariah status of Southern blacks served to create a de facto homogeneity among whites. Jews and Syrians, Germans and Italians all could be classified together in contradistinction to people of African descent. There existed a definitional homogeneity among whites cutting across all other boundaries. This helped to create a greater unity of purpose and value. A most useful means of enhancing group identity is to define one's own against other groups. Southerners not only had the Yankee North; white Southerners had the large Southern black population. Potential intergroup conflict among whites could always be buried under threatened or imagined conflicts between blacks and whites. The appeals for a politically solid South behind the Democratic Party were formed in just such terms.[6]

This is only part of the story. Black Southerners are also Southerners. People who share a society (however inequitably) also participate in (and share) the values and norms of that society. Cultures and societies are the products of unique historical events that are shared by all members of a society or culture, even in the act of negating them. To understand a people one must understand their history—itself a very Southern statement.

Regardless of their attempts to make themselves other than Americans, Southerners' claims to being American extend deep into their history. The South was American before it was Southern. A large percentage of the men responsible for the creation of that which is American, and the United States itself, were from the South. Washington, Jefferson, Madison, and Jackson spring to mind. Yet while Andrew Jackson was in the process of proclaiming the importance and inviolability of union, his fellow Southerners were engaged in creating a history that would set them apart from their fellow citizens. Jackson's conflict with John C. Calhoun over Southern attempts to nullify the federal tariff signified the beginning of differences between the South and the rest of the country, differences formed by opposed sets of interests.

These differences became more pronounced as the agitation over slavery increased and the South felt compelled to defend not only its peculiar institution but also its way of life. As the Northern states became increasingly industrialized during the nineteenth century, they and the Western states desired increasing amounts of internal improvements as well as a national tariff to protect fledgling industries. The South felt threatened and perceived that its position was increasingly tenuous. In addition, growing abolitionist sentiment forced Southerners to articulate a regional distinctiveness. During this time the intellectual forms and structures of Southern life were first elaborated, and they were returned to repeatedly throughout Southern history. They are the virtues of the agrarian life, its necessity for republican government, the view that these United States are a loose confederation of sovereign entities, and the South as the last bastion of constitutional government. It is amusing, almost, to note the similarities between Calhoun's view of nullification and the theories of interposition and the concurrent majority.[7]

The claim of nullification reached its climax in the secession of eleven states from the union and the formation of the Confederate States of America. Their defeat in the war precipitated by that secession was, and is, a dominant event in Southern history. The destruction it caused was a molder of the historical reality of the South in 1930.[8] The War Between the States devastated the South. It determined the economic history of the South in the years following it, as the previous period determined what type of economy would be destroyed.

One-half of the South's farm machinery and one-third of its farm animals were destroyed in the war. The currency of the country was declared void and not redeemed. Not only was the region's infrastructure devastated, but its social and political structures were torn asunder. The elite were disfranchised, many were deprived of their citizenship or imprisoned. Combined with this was the loss of those killed in the war and those who emigrated after it, unable to face the prospect of life in defeat.[9] The states of the former Confederacy were a conquered nation, unwilling hosts to an army of occupation. They were forced to undergo a reconstruction with none of the positive incentives, or results, of those undergone by later defeated countries, for example, Japan and Nazi Germany. No carrot accompanied Reconstruction's stick. The economy lay in ruins, social and political structures in collapse. The unthinkable had happened. The cause was lost indeed, and the "infidel Yankee" and the "barbarian black" were in control. The clouds no longer loomed on the horizon; the whirlwind had arrived.[10]

The forty-seven years between the end of the war and the election of Woodrow Wilson saw four major movements in Southern history: Reconstruction and its aftermath, the emergence of the Populists and the struggle for a new political system, their failure and the resulting disfranchisement of blacks and poor whites, and the development of the New South.

Reconstruction looms in the background of Southern history like a spectre.[11] It was the monster used to frighten children who would not behave. Reconstruction has lingered in the Southern consciousness as a time of unspeakable horrors, or of horrors spoken only in hushed voices. What the Japanese occupation signifies to Koreans. so is Reconstruction to Southerners. Not only was the South a defeated nation, desolate and destroyed, but it was forced to endure the ignominy of an army of occupation and government by carpetbaggers, scalawags, and freedmen. To the Southern mind it remained a time of corrupt government, brigandage, and rapine. It was a time when the most unspeakable of acts in the Southern mind became commonplace—the physical assault upon Southern womanhood by those people whose recent release from the coercive constraints of slavery had caused them to return to

27

that barbarism from which they had only recently been lifted through the ministrations of goodly and upright masters. Regardless of the falsity and absurdity of many of these claims, there was enough truth in some of them—especially that of corruption—and enough fear the others might be true that they became true in people's minds. These fears were a dominant source for Southern attitudes well into the twentieth century and remained influential in 1930. They found their political expression in the Democratic Party in the South as the white man's party. This was strengthened by the Republican Party's willingness to "wave the bloody shirt" in every presidential election, and firmly settled the South as one-third of the epithet hurled at the Democrats as the party of rum, Romanism, and rebellion.

The New South as a historical occurrence can to a great extent be seen as a nonevent. The New South movement was an attempt to industrialize the South and make it more like the North—albeit under the categories of white supremacy. The war and the antebellum South had been, alas, glorious and noble, although lost, causes. They should be remembered as such, and as such promptly forgotten. For the New South all that mattered was the future, and the future in America's Gilded Age was open only to those with money, and money came from industry. The major exponent of the New South was the editor of the *Atlanta Constitution*, Henry Grady, whose speeches and editorials set the tone for Southern economic development. The idea swept the South as people went searching for Northern capital. Communities set about to build their own factories, usually cotton mills, through local investment. Many of these enterprises expired as quickly as they arose. They were killed by ignorance of markets, transportation, and management. Northern investment did come, although in smaller quantities than desired and with results that can be described as no better than mixed.

The movement of Northern industry to the South is a phenomenon not only of the latter half of the twentieth century but of the nineteenth and early twentieth as well. The reasons for both movements are the same—the existence of a fairly docile, because impoverished, work force and the existence of an underclass that could be used to drive wages even lower. This is not to imply that the South was free of labor struggles and violence. The names Harlan, Gastonia, and Birmingham prove otherwise. Still, the South was basically easy pickings for Northern industrialists. This is true not only in terms of labor relations but of society as well.

The impact of Northern capital on the South is an important issue. A major change in the South from 1930 to 1980 was its economic growth and transformation, the movement from poverty to plenty. The New South movement manifested itself in the colonialization of the Southern economy by outside interests. Such a phenomenon is not in itself terrible, but the fruits of that industry were removed from the South. Industries came South to take advantage of the lower wages, yet did not use their lower costs to make local industry more competitive. Instead they structured their marketing in such a way that products manufactured in the South were often more expensive than those produced in the North, despite lower production costs.

C. Vann Woodward has best articulated the view that the South was a colonial economy. In *The Origins of the New South* he argues that the control of raw materials, modes of production, and transportation by outside interests severely curtailed the South's economic development. As an economic colony the South's relation to the North was similar to that of India to England. It supplied raw materials to Northern industry under a controlled pricing system, and then purchased finished materials at inflated prices.

An amazing example of this involves the Union Sulphur Company. Sulphur is a major ingredient of commercial fertilizer. Years of monoculture had seriously depleted the South's soil and in order to maintain production Southern farmers applied large quantities of commercial fertilizer to their land. The average expense for fertilizer was 18 percent of their gross income, between two and three times that for farmers in the rest of the country. Cheap fertilizer would have been, therefore, a great boon. Ninety-five percent of the nation's sulphur deposits were located in Louisiana and Texas. This sulphur could be produced at between $3.75 and $4.50 a ton. Yet it was sold for $18.00 a ton. In 1913 Union Sulphur made a profit of $13.85 a ton and returned $3,700.00 a share. Its annual profits were between 150 and 400 percent of its total investment. These profits were extracted from the Southern farmer just as the sulphur was extracted from the Southern soil.[12]

The story is similar for coal and steel production in Birmingham, which suffered under artificially high prices resulting from its control by United States Steel. Bauxite from Arkansas, coal from Appalachia, oil from Louisiana and Texas, along with wood production and cotton milling were industries with a low value-added ratio. The Northern industrialists who owned most of these Southern industries did not want competition. The South was to be a producer of raw materials to be shipped North, there to be made into finished goods.

Combined with these problems was the control of Southern rail transportation by companies under the domination of J. P. Morgan. The three major carriers in the South—the Atlantic Coast Railroad, the Louisville and Nashville, and the Seaboard Air Line—were all controlled by segments of the Morgan empire. All who used them in the South suffered under freight rate differentials. As early as 1889 the Interstate Commerce Commission held that these differentials were "in a very great degree responsible for the lack of local development in the region, except in favored localities."[13] As late as 1938 shippers in the Southern Territory (the areas between the Atlantic and the Mississippi River, and south of the Ohio and Potomac rivers) paid rates 39 percent higher than those in the official territory. Shippers in the Southwest (Louisiana, Arkansas, Texas, Oklahoma, and part of New Mexico) paid 75 percent more.

While freight rates and price differentials were not the sole reasons for the South's retarded economic development, they definitely affected the South's ability to compete. They also discouraged the location of plants to produce finished goods in the South, where the savings resulting from the proximity of raw materials would be more than offset by the higher prices charged Southern shippers. An example of this is the fixed prices charged for Birmingham iron and steel. In 1924 the Federal Trade Commission determined that the cost of producing steel there was the lowest in the country, 26 percent lower than Pittsburgh. The purchaser of Birmingham steel, however, paid $3.00, and after 1920 $5.00, more per ton than did purchasers of Pittsburgh steel. Steel bars from Pittsburgh were sold at $2.10 above production cost, while those from Birmingham sold for $8.00 over, and Birmingham wire products were sold for $18.30 over the costs of production. As the Federal Trade Commission put it, the steel differential "is retarding not only the growth of consumers in the South but also the producers."[14]

One cannot blame all of the South's economic deficiencies on such artificial constraints. The South suffered from many "natural" difficulties as well. The absence of capital—partially a result of the war—and the scarcity of skilled labor and technical ability, along with a relatively late start in industrialization, served to constrict development. Combined with this were the social structures of an agricultural society that slowed the movement to industrialization. Yet to a great extent Southern agriculture had been in disarray for decades following the Civil War, and the boom period following World War I made the collapse following it even greater. Also, the other problems were not unique to the South. Any society on beginning industrialization finds itself with similar problems. They are usually transitory barriers that can be surmounted given the opportunity. With the existence of external constraints on economic development, however, these natural barriers in the South were intensified. Together they slowed economic development and contributed to making it an economically deprived and poverty stricken region.

The poverty of the South is evident in every economic indicator—per capita wealth, income, bank deposits. And while the South was poor before the Depression, it was even poorer afterward. In 1929 the South's per capita income was $372, compared to $797 for the rest of the country. By 1932 per capita income for the country had dropped to $448, and in the South it had dropped to $203.[15] Whereas in 1929 the per capita income of the South was 47 percent that of the rest of the country, in 1932 it had dropped to 45 percent. Agricultural debt and default rose drastically as the forced sale of farms increased from 21 per thousand in 1927 to 46 per thousand in 1932.[16] In Mississippi the situation was even worse, with forced sales at nearly 100 per thousand and on one day in April 1932 one-quarter of the state was forcibly sold.

State and local government revenues in the South also lagged behind those elsewhere. In 1932 they averaged $33.26 per capita in the South and $69.63 in the rest of the country. As small as that figure may be, it is 48 percent of that for the country as a whole from a region whose per capita income was only 45 percent that of the other states.

As there were reasons for the economic, political, and social situation of the South in 1930, there are reasons for the South's situation in 1980. Some of these are the same; some are radically different. Some are reasonable; some are unreasonable. One is dealing with a people immersed in a society who reflect and create the values of that society. One is also dealing with a subculture, whose members must respond to and internalize the values of the larger society as well. The changes involved, therefore, deal not only with the South but with the wider issues of the United States as a whole.

The year 1930 is an intriguing and interesting date with which to begin a study of the South and social change. Economically, the Depression, which had hit the South earlier and harder than the rest of the country, held everything in its thrall. By 1930 it was an enduring reality. Politically the South was still estranged. With the exception of the South the country had been predominantly Republican since 1860. The political reunification would have to await the election of Franklin Roosevelt in 1932. Then the rest of the country would join the South in voting the Democratic ticket. Socially the South had undergone a very bleak period in the twenties. It had a most negative image in the North, which suffered from a peculiar gullibility: "a

31

volitionless, almost helpless capacity and eagerness," as William Faulkner put it, "to believe anything about the South not even that it be derogatory but merely bizarre enough and strange enough."[17] In the Northern mind the South was a region rampant with racism and Ku Kluxers, malaria and hookworm, poverty and lynchings. A Sahara of the Bozart, as H. L. Mencken called it, "a bunghole of the United States, a cesspool of Baptists, a miasma of Methodism, snake-charmers, phoney real-estate operators, and syphilitic evangelists."[18]

By 1930 only the first two books of what became the Southern literary renaissance had been published. The year 1929 saw the publication of Thomas Wolfe's *Look Homeward, Angel* and William Faulkner's *Sartoris*. The Southern literary emergence lay in the future. The time when a New York editor would plaintively ask "But why Mississippi?" had not yet arrived. Also in 1930 a literary work intended to explode upon the scene appeared. The explosion was smaller than hoped, but its reverberations are still felt. A group of twelve Southern intellectuals contributed to *I'll Take My Stand: The South and the Agrarian Tradition*. Robert Penn Warren, John Crowe Ransom, Allen Tate, Frank Owsley, and others maintained that rampant industrialization and centralization regardless of the form—capitalist, communist, or state socialist—were destructive of the human spirit and humane values. The authors argued that the South's agrarian tradition had given it certain cultural, spiritual, and social strengths inherently necessary to the human spirit. These strengths were threatened by the industrialization and urbanization that had overwhelmed the North and were descending on the South. They claimed there was more to the South than material poverty and the problems endemic to that poverty. Despite economic weaknesses the South had produced a set of religious, cultural, and humane values due to its agrarian tradition. The economic problems of the South, then, could be solved not by industrialization and progress, so called, but by a return to the small farm and by rehabilitating Southern agriculture.[19]

That these men felt compelled to issue such a proclamation at a time when the South was still overwhelmingly rural and agricultural shows their perception of the threat of change. They felt they were offering an alternative to a country suffering from the ill effects of industrialization, as evidenced by the Depression. Their proclamations were ignored. While many of them moved on to formulate the New Criticism and to become preeminent men of letters, their economic theories were forgotten. At the present time, however, John Crowe Ransom's claim resonates. Under industrialization the fight is first of all against nature; they propose to put nature under their heel; this is the dream of the scientists burrowing in their cells, and then of industrial men who beg of their secret knowledge and go out to trouble the earth. But after a certain point this struggle is vain, and we only use ourselves up if we prolong it.[20]

In the period around 1930 the old age was passing away and the new one was yet to be. Allen Tate has suggested this line of reasoning as a possible explanation for the Southern literary renascence. The South was at a crossroads of history. The traditional order was being rapidly obliterated, and a newer order was being born.[21] The next fifty years would see the Southern states undergo if not the most radical, at least the longest-lived, changes in its history.

The South in 1930 was indeed poor, rural, and suffering. The South was also overwhelmingly rural, ranging from a low of 49 percent rural in Florida (five percentage points above the national average, and twenty-one points above the Northeast) to 85 percent in Mississippi. According to the census figures for 1930, only 28.1 percent of the inhabitants of the East South Central states (Kentucky, Tennessee, Alabama, Mississippi) lived in urban areas, and it was only 36.4 percent for the West South Central states (Arkansas, Louisiana, Oklahoma, Texas). Even for the census's South Atlantic grouping the percentage of people living in urban areas was only 36.1, and this value is skewed due to the inclusion of Delaware, Maryland, and the District of Columbia.[22]

By 1930 the Depression had begun to change the fabric of Southern farm society. The drop in cotton prices resulted in a drastic increase in farm foreclosures. The surplus farm population swelled the ranks of Southern tenant farmers and sharecroppers. Between 1920 and 1930 the percentage of Southern farms operated by tenants had increased from 49.6 to 55.5, with a slight decrease to 53.5 percent by 1935. Even this lower number, however, represented 1,831,475 farms. Two-thirds of all of these tenant farmers were white, one-quarter of whom were sharecroppers. One-half of all black tenants were sharecroppers. These tenant families represented 5.5 million white Southerners and 3 million black Southerners. These numbers represented about one-quarter of the South's population. By 1969 these numbers had decreased to 91,693 whites and 16,863 blacks, and by 1970 only 4.6 percent of the South's population lived on farms, and only 35 percent lived in rural areas. This last number constitutes an inversion of the numbers for 1930, when 65 percent of all Southerners lived in rural areas.[23]

These changes in living patterns caused a great deal of change in social structures as well. To a great extent, however, they merely transposed previous structures to a different environment. This is due to the absence of major megalopolises, with the exception of southern Florida and parts of Texas. Movement between country and city remained relatively easy. Also, many Southerners have relatives who continue to live in the rural areas whence many of the urban dwellers only recently removed. In conjunction with this, the towns and cities in the South are smaller than those in the rest of the country. Only 25 percent of all Southerners live in cities with populations over 100,000. In fact South Carolina, Mississippi, and Arkansas had no city over 200,000 as late as 1970.[24]

The movement of Southerners from rural to urban environments indeed altered the social fabric of the South, just as earlier periods of urbanization changed the social structures of New England. The breakdown of social control and the crime, anonymity, and emptiness that so many writers on the city have documented were not unknown in the South.

Urbanization also affected politics. The disproportionate voting strength of rural counties increased with the growth of the cities. These inequalities eventually became so great that the federal courts—despite the political nature of the complaints—felt compelled to enter the conflict and order statewide redistricting.[25] The urbanization of the South affected its politics in other ways as well. Unlike the North, where cities have been the primary political base for blacks, in the South it has been those rural counties with a predominantly black population. The cities have provided, however, a base for black and white moderate coalitions. They have also been an increasingly strong base for Republican forays. People upon leaving the city and moving to the suburbs increasingly identify with the Republican Party.

Urbanization transformed the work force. As Southerners left the farms and moved to cities and towns their means of livelihood changed. They ceased to be farmers or suppliers of goods to farmers, and became involved in manufacturing and service industries. With the advent of World War II, large numbers of military bases were built in the South. This development, the result of the South's relatively mild climate and the seniority of its senators and representatives, also brought an influx of jobs and capital.

Growth in Southern industry, and the resulting change in the work force, owed much to technological innovations and discoveries. One of the most important was the discovery of how to make paper from wood fibers. As a result, two new industries arose in the South—the growing and harvesting of pulpwood and the milling of paper.

Technological innovations were equally responsible for the changes in agriculture. The discovery of myriad uses for peanuts, the eradication of most epidemic animal diseases, refrigerated trucking, and the improvement of the highway system resulted in crop diversification, cattle and chicken production, and the Florida citrus crop. As cotton ceased to be king, the introduction of the mechanical cotton picker reduced even further the number of people necessary for its harvesting—just as other mechanical devices decreased the number of people required for the entire growing process. This lowered the number of people needed in the farming industry and both freed and required people to search for work in other sectors.

Developments in transportation and communication transformed the social makeup and organization of the South, just as they did the country at large. The transportation shift in the South came about with the increasing availability of automobiles and the growth of paved roads. Along with this, the massive amounts of money put into the federal highway system unified the country on a physical level. Accompanying this ease of mobility was a reduction in the rootedness of people to a particular place. Travel between sections eased feelings of difference that traditionally pervaded dealings between the North and the South. It also made relocation easier. Here the fusion of several changes occasioned an occurrence of great social import.

Urbanization, industrialization, and increased ease of mobility were both cause and effect in transforming traditional Southern patterns of birth, life, and death occurring in a geographically isolated region. The nature of these relationships is seen in urbanization's requirement that people live in proximity to one another and in the way continued urbanization acts as a magnet to individuals looking for employment and other opportunities. There is increasing initiative to relocate when the number of jobs in agriculture is decreasing or the jobs are no longer appealing.

Industrialization too requires the presence of a number of people in a particular area. As a result, urbanization and industrialization tend to occur together. Simultaneously both draw large numbers of people to them, just as they require large numbers to exist.

Telecommunication has had an even greater impact on the South and its inhabitants than did the developments in transportation. Radio and television in the United States have been dominated by the Northeast and California, which have determined the norms for family life, social behavior, and the social

35

environment. To a great extent the picture coming from the television impressed upon Southerners their differences from what was normal and their inferior status as viewed by the North. As Blanche McCrary Boyd has put it:

> I started wanting to leave the South when I was eight years old and we got a television. We got our set before the Charleston station actually opened, so I spent hours staring at the station logo. . . .
>
> When the logo disappeared and television programs appeared in its place, a dreadful truth came clear to me: Southerners were not normal people. We did not sound like normal people, or have the same style of physical movement. What we chose to talk about seemed peculiarly different also. I began to realize we were hicks.
>
> It was a lot for an eight year old to deal with; I was already suspicious because of basements and snow. We didn't have any snow in South Carolina, and in school the textbooks showed beautiful pictures of neighborhoods covered with icing. And I knew normal houses had basements. Even the houses in the Dick and Jane books had basements. But since Charleston was ocean-bottom flat, homes were flush with the ground. Television confirmed my suspicions and took away my faith in my surroundings. I didn't want to be a hick.[26]

This phenomenon was not limited to the early days of television in the 1950s; it was dominant throughout the 1960s and 1970s, and even into the 1980s. Shows constantly showed Southerners, and rural inhabitants in general, as idiots and buffoons. They were upright and virtuous buffoons, perhaps, but still abnormal and strange. Roy Blount best summed the attitude of the national media to the South in the title of an article he wrote for *TV Guide*, "C'mon, They're Not All Dumber Than Two-Dollar Dogs."[27]

Television and radio have served, nonetheless, as instruments tying the South more closely to the rest of the country and decreasing certain forms of Southern distinctiveness. A notable example is the dearth of Southern (or other) accents among television announcers, with the singular exceptions of Bill Moyers and Jim Lehrer. This results in the creation of a normative form of speech, not unlike BBC English. It is not necessarily the way people do speak, but is presented as the way people should speak.

The telecommunications media also bring the various regions of the country closer. Events occurring in one part of the country are not noticeably separated in time from their presentation in another part of the country. Not only were events in the rest of the country and the world made present to the South, but events in the South could be made known to those living outside of it. If necessary people could respond to those events with a relative degree of immediacy.[28]

It is in this overturning of political and social structures that the changes in the South have been most visible, most hard fought, and most public. While those changes have not necessarily had the greatest impact on the lives of white Southerners, they exerted a particular dominance over the history of the region. To a great extent this results from the fact that nearly all changes in the political structure relate in some way to changes in race relations. From the mid-forties to the mid-seventies integration and the dismantling of institutionalized white supremacy dominated the Southern political arena. State and local governments expended a great deal of energy in futile efforts to evade the laws of the land. Violence and threats of violence permeated many states, and at least one Southern politician became a legitimate presidential contender due to his opposition to integration. To a great extent white Southerners have not considered blacks as actors on the historical stage but instead as props that are acted upon. Their parts have been written for them.

In the fifty-year period from 1930 to 1980 this changed drastically and radically. The earlier movements for civil rights began to bear fruit. The region and the country found themselves transformed. The first major steps in this direction occurred during and following World War I. Troop mobilization transported large numbers of Southern blacks into Northern states and European countries, especially France, where color prejudice was different from that at home. It also removed them from a great number of constraints they had lived under. Wartime saw the beginning of the migration of Southern blacks to the North. This resulted from the burgeoning war industries, and continued after the war. These occurrences revealed to blacks, especially Southern blacks, the vivid reality that social structures did not only not have to be the way they were, but that in some areas they were already better. Chicago certainly was not perfect, but it was better than Mississippi—at least most of the time.

The year 1930 can be seen as a kind of watershed in race relations. The early decades of the twentieth century, and especially the 1920s, were a period of racial conflict that saw a resurgence of the Ku Klux Klan. Yet 1930 also saw a resurgence of black activism over an attempted appointment by President Hoover. Judge John J. Parker of North Carolina, Hoover's nominee to the Supreme Court, was challenged on the basis of his statement that black participation in politics "was a source of evil and danger."[29] After Judge Parker refused to respond to inquiries about the statement the NAACP mounted a campaign conducted "with a snap, determination, and intelligence never surpassed in colored America, and very seldom in white."[30] While the defeat of Parker in the Senate by a 41-39 vote was the result of several factors, it operated to "give the American Negro a consciousness of his voting power."[31]

Despite the continued failure of the Senate to pass a federal antilynching law, the numbers of lynchings in the South, and the country, continued to decline throughout the 1930s to a total of three in 1938. There are many reasons for this decrease, not the least was the work of the Commission on Inter-racial Cooperation and the Association of Southern Women for the Prevention of Lynching. Both of these groups were comprised of Southerners dedicated to the easing of racial tensions, the development of racial harmony, and the mitigation of the constraints under which blacks lived and labored. Other factors in decreasing racial violence were the continued threat of a federal antilynch law, better roads and communications, the development of state police systems, and the increasingly critical attitude of Southern newspapers.

The 1930s also saw a shift in black voting patterns away from the party of Lincoln into the Democratic Party, where they constituted a part of the New Deal coalition. As a result of this shift, and the ability of blacks to pursue their political goals through the courts, the period between 1930 and 1980 saw a dismantling of de jure segregation and a partial end to de facto segregation. What was the social system in the South in 1930? The facts of the Jim Crow South is an insufficient answer. What is most important is the perception of reality by white Southerners. What was the reality they saw, and what did it mean for it to change? To a great extent this is a "white" story, for the members of the Southern Baptist Convention are an overwhelmingly white group. It would be more true to say that the picture is similar to an Escher print, which at first glance appears to be a series of white figures outlined in black, but upon closer inspection shows itself to be a series of black figures outlined in white. Both are necessary for the composition of the picture, and one can be seen only due to the existence of the other. Such is the story of blacks and whites in the South.

The racial system in the American South, the legal and social structures of Jim Crow, did not emerge complete with the arrival of blacks in the American colonies. Nor did it appear in its completeness with the demise of Reconstruction and the removal of federal troops from the South. The development of Jim Crow laws, as Woodward has shown, was an event of historical becoming. Each law was a response to new social, economic, and technological realities. These laws were expanded and elaborated upon as late as the 1930s and 1940s. The 1944 act in Virginia empowering the State Corporation Commission to require separate waiting rooms and other facilities in airports is an example. The Jim Crow South was a world of racial divisions, of separate waiting rooms, rest rooms, water fountains, taxicabs, and seating on buses. All of these were legislatively mandated, with the required signs proclaiming "white" or "colored" over the respective facility. The signs were practically unnecessary since the mere appearance of the facility was sufficient to proclaim for which race it was intended. The complexity resulting from such a situation can perhaps best be seen in the absurdities to which they gave rise, such as an ordinance passed in Birmingham, Alabama, in 1930 making it "unlawful for a Negro or a white person to play together or in company with each other" at dominoes or checkers.[32] Lillian Smith tells of those Southern towns too poor to afford more than one public water fountain, which they duly labeled white on one side and colored on the other. This was the type of situation dictated to people too good to deny blacks a drinking fountain, as some communities did, but too cowardly to dispense with the ritual.[33]

The legally mandated social segregation was matched by the political disfranchisement of Southern blacks. As J. Morgan Kousser has shown, this was accomplished along with the disfranchisement of poorer whites.[34] Not only was black voting lowered to almost zero—with the exceptions of certain urban areas and areas where black voters were useful to the political machine, for example, Memphis—it also made white voting the lowest in the country.[35] The machinery of white supremacy required a great deal of political and mental effort, effort that could have been used to alleviate the poverty, ill health, and poor education that haunted the South. While some politicians, such as Theodore Bilbo, could combine progressive, even radical, political outlooks with the most vituperative racism, often the language of white supremacy was a smokescreen to hide political failures and inaction. A story told by Albert Brewer illustrates this. While serving as George Wallace's handpicked speaker in the Alabama State House, Brewer went to offer sympathy to Wallace, then governor, over a recently passed tax bill that he had opposed during the election. Wallace, who would sign the bill, simply looked up and said, "I'll just holler 'nigger' and everybody will forget it."[36]

While it is obvious that such a system could tear into the psyches of blacks, the impact on whites is too easily overlooked.[37] Robert Coles gives a poignant and direct example of the impact segregation had on the white psyche in his discussion of the relationship between James Butler and Butler's brother. The

Butlers were a wealthy Alabama family. James was a physician, his brother a lawyer and a professor of law. In 1965, after the passage of the Civil Rights Act, James initiated a movement to desegregate the facilities of the two hospitals on whose staffs he served. He also signed a public statement of support for the new law. For doing this James Butler became a pariah, a subject for attack and ostracism. Among those who treated him so were his brother, his friends, and most of his colleagues. As he put it, "I became a radical to people hungry for one. In a way I think they were very grateful to me. It can be a relief to find a real human object for all your hates and fears. The communist under the bed, in the shadows, up in New York and abroad stop satisfying even the most paranoid person's sense of reality after a while."[38]

Butler continues, showing how an already damaged psyche could, and easily did, rupture at the slightest attack upon the bastions of white supremacy.

> The worst part was my brother's reaction. We were never exceptionally close, but neither were we unfriendly. The strangest part of all this is that I was our Negro nurse's favorite, and only realized that fact during my analysis. . . . The nurse really was our mother, until we were sent off to school after twelve. Naturally, my brother went to school first, being older. He would come home on holidays full of jokes about niggers, how stupid they are and animal-like. I never connected his attitude then with the fact that I was alone with Ruth, and he away from her. In his heart he must have felt the way I did when I finally did leave—homesick, and more for our nurse Ruth and handyman John than either of us dared admit to ourselves, let alone anyone else.
>
> When my brother became so angry at me, and started calling me "a god-damned nigger lover," I asked why he was so excited, just because—in 1964, mind you—I was advocating what the United States Congress had long since proclaimed law. He said I had always been "soft on niggers," and maybe I should go North where I seemed to belong. I couldn't get him to talk any more rationally than that, and he is a lawyer, an Ivy League-trained lawyer.
>
> . . . A lot of us in Alabama shout at niggers because we're afraid not to shout, or because it's like owning a car or a house or *something*; you feel you are somebody when you can do it, or join others who are doing it.[39]

John Howard Griffin's *Black Like Me* shows more fully how the social system could warp and deprave. While whites would rarely pick up Griffin when he hitchhiked during the day, he readily got rides after dark. He described one night of hitchhiking along the Gulf Coast of Mississippi.

> It became quickly obvious why they picked me up. All but two picked me up the way they would pick up a pornographic photograph or book—except that

40

this was verbal pornography. With a negro they assumed they need give no semblance of self-respect or respectability.

. . . Some were shamelessly open, some shamelessly subtle. All showed morbid curiosity about the sexual life of the Negro, and all had at base, the same stereotyped image of the Negro as an inexhaustible sex-machine with oversized genitals and a vast store of experiences, immensely varied.

. . . I note these things because it is harrowing to see decent-looking men and boys assume that because a man is black they need show him none of the reticences they would, out of respect, show the most derelict white man. . . . [A]ll that I could see were men shorn of respect either for themselves or their companion.[40]

For the South and Southerners, both black and white, white supremacy was a fact. It was an overwhelming social and political reality that demanded an entire series of responses. These responses were internalized to such a degree that their manifestation was immediate and unreflective. Politesse did not require that one call blacks Mr., Mrs., or Miss, but tradition required that one call them by their first name or at most Uncle or Aunt. At the lowest level every black male became John, or boy. It required of blacks the ability to step off sidewalks quickly as whites approached, not to stare too directly in the faces of whites, and not to desire too much from the white world. It required of whites the constant manifestations of the reality of black inferiority, the knowledge that blacks must be kept constantly in their place if racial harmony were to be maintained.

This was the great irony of the situation. Most Southern whites felt that there was no racial problem. Southerners understood and loved their black population, and knew that blacks were content with their situation. Problems arose only when outside influences came into the community, outside agitators who brought alien and inappropriate ideas into a complacent and contented community in order to stir up trouble. This is what white Southerners thought, or thought they thought. The reasons this had to be claimed, had to be true in their minds, are readily ascertainable. The institutional structures of white supremacy were an integral part of the identification of Southerners. Members of the community held it to be valid, good, correct. Communities, like individuals, do not hold beliefs that they know (or admit) to be wrong. If the structures of white supremacy were correct there had to be within them an element of equitability for both groups. This is to say that regardless of the apparent inequality of the relationship, the inequality was somehow equitable. The situation was required to be that way, regardless of whether that requirement resulted from the inherent genetic inferiority of blacks, some God-

41

ordained reality, or the cultural backwardness of blacks who might someday be ready for equality but were not at present. In the Southern mind this equity had to be recognized by blacks as well as whites. This explains the point raised consistently by white Southerners that the Southern black was content and did not desire any change in the situation. That white Southerners could believe this, or act as though they did, says a great deal for the potential for self-delusion. People are readily convinced of that which they want to believe. It also says a great deal about the myopia of dominant groups when it comes to analyzing and grasping the reality over which they dominate.

THREE

The Idea of Southernness

That the Southern states have a peculiar and unique history setting them apart from the rest of the United States has been illustrated. Historical events alone, however, make neither a culture nor a society. The distinctiveness of the American South resides not so much in its unique history per se but in the cultural forms resulting from the internalization of that history. It is incorrect, therefore, to think of the South, or the Southerner, as having been a place or an individual existing wholly formed at one time. As Louis Rubin has phrased it, "at no time was there ever a static, changeless society known as the South, inhabited by fully-realized, timeless human exemplars known as southerners, for whom there was no problem of self-definition in changing times."[1] Those who have claimed that the South existed as a result of a particular entity, be it slavery or agrarianism or white supremacy, have been proven wrong. Industrialism no more destroyed the South as a society than did the Thirteenth Amendment or integration. And why should it have done so? The industrialization of Japan, Russia, and the Union of South Africa did not destroy Japanese, Russian, or Boer cultures.[2] Certainly all changed as a result, but their responses to and manipulation of the forms of industrialization were unique to their societies and their cultures.

Certain traditional ways of perceiving the South view it as being somehow an illegitimate society, existing only because of one or more perverse characteristics the removal of which would make the South more normal, more like the rest of the country—which, after all, is wanted anyway. Such thinking is illustrative of the claim by Jonathan Daniels that "Southerners are a mythological people, created half out of dream and half out of slander, who live in a still legendary land."[3]

What is of interest is less an examination of the South than of the Southerner and the idea of Southernness. A social and cultural ethos was created by the responses of a people to their unique experience of history. Just as it was important to examine the historical changes in the South in order to see what Southern Baptists responded to in this period, it is equally important to examine the cultural milieu in order to grasp the sources and attitudes of the region they inhabited.

The understanding of the South, therefore, must not be seen only in its history, although history has dominated and even tyrannized it. The South's culture and society were created by a people's internalization of material realities wrought by historical, social, and economic forces. As George B. Tindall has phrased it, "The lessons that southerners in the large have derived from their history—or rather from their communal heritage—are not properly speaking, lessons at all so much as formative influences which have shaped their identity."[4] Among these people there are indeed many differences, yet the similarities between the various Souths are sufficient to hold them together as a unit for comparison to the rest of the United States. This is illustrated by Reynolds Price.

> The South is a country larger than France; and I can travel from Durham, North Carolina to Jackson, Mississippi, which is a distance of 800 miles, and find that people are still speaking almost exactly the same dialect that I have grown up with and known all my life, whereas I can go from Durham, North Carolina to Philadelphia, a distance of 400 miles, and find them speaking an utterly different dialect. . . . So it's not so much a matter of geographical distance as it is of a prevailing tradition over a large part of the country.[5]

The South is an entity distinctive and recognizable. It is not to be confused with facts, nor limited to its history. In some respects Southerners' self-perceptions as different from the rest of the country are increasing.[6] George Tindall quotes Jonathan Daniels again: "For good or for ill, being a Southerner is like being a Jew." Tindall continues this thought, "And, indeed, more needs to be written of the similarity of the minds and the emotions of the Jew, the Irishman, the Southerner, and, perhaps, the Pole, as a basis for the better understanding of each of them and of them all."[7] To speak of the South in terms of certain characteristics, especially characteristics based on historical realities such as white supremacy, traditionalism, and ruralism fails to explain why a culture continues to survive after the claimed defining characteristic no longer exists. It would be better just to paraphrase Irving Babbitt's observation of the Spanish, "there seems to be something southern about southerners that causes them to behave in a southern manner," and leave it at that.[8]

If, as some have said, being a Southerner is a "spiritual condition, like being a [pre-Vatican II] Catholic, or a Jew," then one should look to that spiritual condition in order to discover the sources of Southernness. But for the South this spirit cannot be its dominant religious body, although it participates greatly in it. The structures of the Southern Baptist Convention finally prevent it from making the final leap as cultural church, although it often finds itself inextricably entwined in the web of that culture. The churches of the South fundamentally cannot fill the void that Roman Catholicism does for the Poles, or Judaism, however secularized, does for the Jews. In this aspect Southerners are much closer to the Irish; in having suffered they have "in a way made a religion of [their] history."[9]

I therefore examine the nature of Southernness as manifested in its literature. The literary "truths," if I may, of Southern literature illuminate an internal strength of Southern society and Southern culture. Simultaneously the particular forms of that literature, and its ability to express those truths, result from the unique elements in the history of the American South. Woodward suggests that the strength of Southern novelists resides in their ability to grasp the fundament of Southern society while expressing universal truths.

> They too wrote about the past, the Southern past, or more typically the past in the present. But the best of them clearly labored under no vows to justify or celebrate any past or present they wrote about. They might conjure up the past to illuminate, to explain, or to give meaning to the present, but not to vindicate it. The characters they created betrayed no need for heroes or villains on the part of their creators; and the stories they told were shaped by no creed and illustrated no theory about past, present, or future. Their example did not encourage sociological generalization about types, classes, races—planters, yeomen, poor whites, or slaves—but rather supported the historian's concern for the particular, the concrete, the individual. Most important of all was the proof so magnificently presented in their work that the provincial subject matter we shared was no trap of obscurity but an embarrassment of riches, a treasure of neglected opportunity.[10]

This does not imply that all of these sources have been positive and uplifting. Indeed, they have not been. In fact it might be that because Southerners were the only (white) Americans to have experienced defeat and tragedy, as well as overwhelming guilt and responsibility, its citizens have been able to write their particular fiction.

The South is very much a culture based on the story, on the relating of events from one person to another. This inherently Southern characteristic is shared by black and white. Ralph Ellison and Richard Wright must be considered great Southern writers just as much as William Faulkner, Robert

Penn Warren, and Eudora Welty. To extend the earlier analogy, the story is something else that Southerners share with the Irish and the Jews. There is a desire to tell, to share experience, and to pass on knowledge. Southern literature is inherently immersed in a history, a community, and a people.

Even a character as bereft of roots as Joe Christmas appears to be in William Faulkner's *Light in August* finds himself immersed in a history of his birth, life, and eventual death because of who he is and whence he comes. It is possible to attribute the sources of catastrophe in the novel to Lena, whose behaviors are ungrounded because she has no fundamental human ties to those around her. To pick up and go does not free one in the Southern novel. There exists no faith in the Great Geography as the solution for all problems. Indeed, to cut oneself loose from one's community, family, and sources is to open the way for destruction and despair. The story is repeated as much in high culture as it is in low culture—the novel and the country song. The characters in the dominant modes of Southern literature are always related, or at least should be. If in some way the relations are incomplete or broken, tragedy results. The same set of relational elements guides the characters themselves, setting them within a vortex of historical, familial, and communal structures from which they cannot escape. Often these structures overwhelm the characters. History catches up to them and destroys them, just as it destroys Thomas Sutpen and his family in *Absalom, Absalom!* The way literature metaphorically reproduces Southern reality is nearly too obvious to note. The sins of the fathers visit themselves upon all subsequent generations just as much as upon the sinners themselves.

Related to this is the refusal of the Southern writer to admit to any simple resolution of problems, or (perhaps) any resolution at all. In a review of *Absalom, Absalom!,* comparing it to the novels of the industrial Northeast at that time (1936), one critic stated that the greatest difference was that the "revolutionary novels" of the period were "very soothing because they give us the sense that men and women are tamed creatures who can easily be made satisfied with bread and circuses and with easy sensual gratification." With the transformation of economic structures, "the incompleteness of human nature can be made complete." To her, however, Faulkner's novels were

> very disturbing because they give us the sense that human beings will never be satisfied with anything that society can give them, that they are so tortuous, so mutually destructive, and so self-destructive that there is no possibility of any social change making very much difference in human existence.[11]

What then are the themes or attitudes in Southern literature that are representative of Southernness and that reflect Southern culture? They are ✓ history, religion, guilt, responsibility, and community. To these are related defeat, relatedness, and personalism.[12] These attitudes are interrelated, emerging from and calling forth one another. Guilt and defeat flow into responsibility. The relatedness of the individual to others (personalism) emerges from the location of the individual as a member of a community to which she or he is responsible. Over all of these structures are history and religion, the latter not creedal but exceedingly spiritual.

Flannery O'Connor, responding to the question why there was an abundance of freaks in Southern literature, answered that it was because "we are still able to recognize one." She continued:

> To be able to recognize a freak you have to have some conception of the whole man, and in the South the general conception of man is still, on the whole, theological. . . . I think it is safe to say that while the South is hardly Christ centered it is most certainly Christ haunted. The Southerner who isn't convinced of it, is very much afraid that he may have been formed in the image and likeness of God.[13]

This spirit looms over Southern literature, where it competes with history as the source of all answers, or all problems. The South is indeed a God- ✓ haunted culture, living with guilt, sin, and the possibility—though rarely visible in most writers—of hope. The hope as seen by the Southern writer is a theological vision, or perhaps as Louis Rubin puts it, a religious vision. For him this means "that the image of human life that it represents is one in which the values embodied in it—love and honor and pity and pride and compassion and sacrifice, to adopt Faulkner's memorable assessment—have not been relativistic, arbitrary, materialistic, but absolute, unswerving, spiritual."[14]

Theology in most Southern literature is apophatic. The negatives offer the possibility of something different. The freaks, the deformed, and the maimed in the novels of Flannery O'Connor bespeak the possibility of wholeness while proclaiming their corruption. The *idea* of a wholeness remains, although the reality of it has disappeared. The tomb might be empty but its very emptiness manifests the possibility of resurrection. The Southern writer, just like the Southerner, has not yet walked upon the road to Emmaus nor placed her hand in the nail-scarred hand. The vision of wholeness has not yet appeared, but its possibility remains.

47

If the vision of hope is always latent, the knowledge of sin is always immanent. The experience of sin and guilt—personal, communal, and historical—is constant. From Flannery O'Connor's freaks, to Robert Penn Warren's Percy Munn in *Night Rider*, to William Styron's Sophie the guilty nature of humans is disclosed, more subtly in some than in others.[15] O'Connor's characters carry their fallenness about with them, they wear it as a badge. Human depravity manifests itself materially and visually. We find in her novels a medieval morality play where the characters wear their failings and their sins as part of their costume. In Warren's and Styron's novels the "sins" of the characters are somewhat less visible but no less complex. Percy Munn finds himself caught in a whirlwind of social and personal choices that lead eventually to the loss of his wife, estate, and finally his life. Before this, however, he is reduced to living in a cave, emerging only at night—leaving darkness for darkness. It matters not (or does it?) that the source of these occurrences appears to have been good decision—his involvement with an association of tobacco growers trying to get higher prices for their produce.[16] But his failure to reject violence, and his eventual commitment to it (hence the title *Night Rider*), results in his destruction. For the major Southern writers it is moral failure, however small, that eventuates in the destruction of the character, whether it be at the hands of others, or by one's own hand as is the case in *Sophie's Choice*. Most tragic, however, is that there often is no escape from the moral decision that produces the tragic result. This is illustrated most vividly in the haunting choice into which Sophie was forced.

The results of this guilt are not solely visited upon the source of the sin. In the Southern novel, as in Southern history itself, guilt passes down from one generation to the next. In Faulkner's *Absalom, Absalom!* the actions of Thomas Sutpen eventuate in homicide, insanity, arson, and fratricide all passing through several generations. Thomas Sutpen emerges in the beginning as an innocent. He comes from nowhere: he has no roots and, evidently, no history. He builds a mansion, takes a bride, and builds (or intends to build) a dynasty. History, his history, catches up with him, however. His refusal to accept this history sets in motion the series of events that end in destruction. His actions set loose a series of events that conspire to destroy him and all that he holds to be important. That the events in the novel are closely related to slavery, miscegenation, and racism brings the impact closer to home. Events have repercussions beyond what could be visible to the actors. The refusal to admit one's sins, to set them right, so to speak—in the case of the novel, to own up to one's children—results in the destruction of a family and a world.

Death is not even the end, only total destruction will suffice—such as the fire that finally destroys Sutpen's Hundred.

Guilt in Southern literature is not only, or even primarily, individual. Guilt, like one's life, is always historical and relational. History as the story of eventualities dominates the Southern mind. This does not mean that Southerners are more historically aware than other Americans, only that the experience of history as a lived reality through its results affects Southerners differently from other Americans, especially Northern and Western white Americans. "To be a southerner today is still to be heir to a complex set of attitudes and affinities, assumptions and instincts, that are the product of history acting upon geography, even though much of the history is now forgotten and the geography modified."[17] White Southerners have experienced American history in a way that is unique among white Americans.

> Southern history, unlike American, includes large components of frustration, failure, and defeat. It includes not only an overwhelming military defeat but long decades of defeat in the provinces of economic, social, and political life. Such a heritage affords the Southern people no basis for the delusion that there is nothing whatever beyond their power to accomplish.[18]

History, therefore, is not an academic enterprise in the Southern mind. It is a reality, the results of which are constantly present. From the presence of the South's black population, through its relative poverty, to the fact that it is attached to a country that defeated it in a war, the South and white Southerners live daily the history of their region, live daily with the actions of their ancestors, and struggle for responses to the legacy that has been bequeathed them. History in the American South is inextricably linked with guilt and responsibility. It also unites the dead and the living in a bond that neither is capable of removing. This is recognized even by those who have no connection with the South, and is illustrated even by Arnold Toynbee regarding Queen Victoria's Diamond Jubilee.

> I remember the atmosphere. It was: well, here we are on the top of the world, and we have arrived at this peak to stay there—forever! There is of course, a thing called history, but history is something unpleasant that happens to other people. We are comfortably outside all that. I am sure, if I had been a small boy in New York in 1897 I should have felt the same. Of course if I had been a small boy in 1897 in the Southern part of the United States I should not have felt the same; I should have known from my parents that history had happened to my part of the world.[19]

49

Whether it is the decadence of a Tennessee Williams play or a Truman Capote short story, the tragedy of a Faulkner or Warren novel, this awareness of the past in the present dominates. The novelists themselves are aware of this. It is seen in Faulkner's epigram, "The past isn't dead. It isn't even past," and the closing lines of Robert Penn Warren's *All the King's Men*, ". . . soon now we shall go out of the house and go into the convulsion of the world, out of history into history and the awful responsibility of Time."[20] In this attitude Southern authors represent the reality of their place. It is also, for all intents and purposes, a universal reality.[21]

History has happened to the South. As Southerners live with the repercussions of that history they relive the errors and evils—as well as the strength and decency—of their forebears. They carry the burden of guilt passed down from one generation to the next. It matters not whether this guilt is admitted; it is imposed. History is always present for Southerners, from the legacy of slavery to what Faulkner has called the chance

> . . . of every Southern boy fourteen years old, not once but whenever he wants it, there is the instant when it's still not yet two oclock on that July afternoon in 1863, the brigades are in position behind the rail fence, the guns are laid and ready in the woods and the furled flags are already loosened to break out . . . and it's all in the balance, it hasn't happened yet, it hasn't even begun yet, it not only hasn't begun yet but there is still time for it not to begin against that position and those circumstances . . . yet it's going to begin, we all know that, we have come too far with too much at stake and that moment doesn't need even a fourteen-year-old boy to think *This time. Maybe this time* with all this much to lose and all this much to gain: Pennsylvania, Maryland, the world, the golden dome of Washington itself to crown with desperate and unbelievable victory the desperate gamble, the cast made two years ago.[22]

History and guilt flow into the Southern reality as relational. One has a place, a community, and a family, and a position in all of these. While the relations one has with one's place and family might cause problems, the absence of relations causes destruction. In fact the possibility of such absence is itself a delusion. History returns to haunt one, and if Joe Christmas in *Light in August* is any example, attempts to run away lead one deeper into the vortex of relationships and responsibilities. The Southerner is aware of being constantly immersed in a particular community to which she or he owes . . . something. This something is so primordial as to be beyond words and description. Yet it is there, and it haunts the Southerner. This involvement of the individual with community does not suggest a completely agreeable and harmonious world. What is often manifested in the writing is the desire, even the need, to escape and the inability to do so. One need only recall that Huck and Jim in their attempts to escape to the North find themselves moving deeper and deeper into the South. The raft and the river that should be the sources of their freedom carry them farther and farther into responsibility and involvement, and metaphorically even deeper into their community.

Two different writers illustrate the impact of community on the individual. One is the recollection of an actual occurrence, the other a literary exercise on the importance of humor in Southern life. Both illustrate the inability of the Southerner to separate from her or his world. These stories exemplify the problems involved for Southern Baptists and all Southerners in challenging the accepted values of their community. The awareness of one's responsibility to others is very strong in the South. How could one hurt and challenge those one loves and who care for one? That is the fundamental pathos. The need and desire to belong, the inability not to belong, the awareness of one's responsibility to those around one, and the fear of destroying that fragile reality known as human community are themes dominating the literature of the South. Tragedy emerges from the fact that responsible moral action demands that one, as a free moral agent, challenge that community on occasion, while the challenge itself is simultaneously an affront to morality. To quote Louis Rubin:

> The evidence of Southern literature, it seems to me . . . is that in every time and place men have faced the task of reconciling individual and private virtue with an inescapable need for fulfillment within a community of men and women, and there is always the requirement to redefine the ethical and moral assumptions of one's rearing and one's present social circumstance amid change.[23]

The examples I will discuss are less filled with tragedy; they call forth good times among friends and family. The first is a story by Louis Rubin about an evening spent with John Donald Wade, two other nationally known Southern academics, and a Northern colleague. The second is an essay by John Donald Wade himself.

Rubin recalls the course of a relaxed evening of conversation, aided by alcohol. The conversation between

> Mr. Wade and his friends obviously fascinated my [Yankee] friend. Their stories, and the way they told them, were stories about people around home. They told these stories in good southern fashion, with lots of drawling and contracting of

syllables—and if you hadn't known that the storytellers consisted of a distinguished literary scholar and editor, a distinguished historian, and a distinguished economist, you might have thought they were members of the local farming community thereabouts.[24]

On leaving for the evening, Rubin's Yankee friend expressed his astonishment. "Why did you *hear* them? Going on like that, talking like *countrymen?* . . . Why you would never have *guessed* who they *were!*" Rubin was not surprised; he was aware of what was happening. They were "demonstrating to each other, but most of all to themselves, that they were still southern boys." They were "asserting their community identity." Certainly they had gone away to college and graduate school and become scholars, but their academic endeavors did not seem quite real to them even yet. They remembered a different sort of community, a different kind of reality, "in which individual people were considered more important than ideas and in which the participants were not set off into academic disciplines and professions and economic brackets, but were part of a society made up of various kinds of men and women with all kinds of jobs and interests and levels of education." All three of the gentlemen remembered that earlier society and the type of identity it afforded its members. They missed it and each could, over a drink with old friends, "reassert that earlier identity" and show that "he was still part of it and it was still part of him."[25]

Rubin's Yankee friend, however, was baffled by this behavior, feeling no such inclinations himself. Being a scholar and university professor was sufficiently satisfying that he craved no further "real life." The Southern academics, however, remembered something different, which called back to them from another time. Despite having separated themselves from it, somehow it still held them, and guilt at having left it nagged at them.

This attitude finds a more literary form in John Donald Wade's essay on Southern humor. Wade creates an imaginary Christmas dinner in 1932. The dinner is populated with friends and family: a farmer, a letter carrier, a physician, a local merchant, a lawyer. Also in attendance are a cousin who is a curator of an art gallery in Chicago, a professor of French at Vassar, and a young scholar just back from Oxford. While the setting and the characters are imaginary, many of the latter are drawn from real life. There is a John (John Crowe Ransom), a Red (Robert Penn Warren), an Andrew (Andrew Lytle), and others. Somehow all of these guests are supposed to carry on an enjoyable and pleasant dinner together. Conversation is to fulfill this task. There must, therefore, be something to link together this disparate group. "Would it do, here, for Cousin Julius to talk of Proust's analyses, for Cousin Mary to tell of Epstein . . . ?" Wade asks. He quickly answers his own question: "It would never, never do." The characters relate to each other through the telling of stories, stories that "mail-carrying Uncle Jack and Proust-teaching Cousin Julius will both think pointed." Wade admits that he wants to show that there is a fundamental link among all the participants. This is the existence of a social tradition, "which insists that human beings must remain humorous . . . if they are to remain human, and one may well believe that it will reassert itself."[26]

Rubin, in his interpretation of the essay sees another meaning, a meaning not dissimilar to that of his own story. According to Rubin, Wade was attempting to show, for example, that despite the fact that one of the guests (Warren) had recently returned from a year in England, his fundamental identity and kinship "did not lie in his intellectual Oxford identity but in that which he shared with the farmer and mail carrier." The Southerner as intellectual could do whatever she or he wished—even study Proust—"but what joined him with the other people who mattered was not the Proust but the story about the plain folk."[27]

Wade is attempting to show the validity of his understanding of Southern society as an organic whole. The Proust scholar was "equally at home with and valued with the lawyer, the doctor, the merchant, the farmer, the mail carrier."[28] Wade has an ideological ax to grind, but whether or not we agree with his claim that the Southern intellectual must retrieve the tradition "by violence" and return to that organic society through an act of will, that this appears necessary illustrates the hold that society and culture have on the individual's psyche. Belonging to the community is seen as imperative and difference is somehow guilt-provoking—sufficiently so to cause an attempt to retrieve it through an act of will. These claims illumine the reluctance of the majority of Southerners fundamentally to challenge the values of their community, as well as why they are so prone to react defensively to attack. An attack on one's community is tantamount to an attack on one's own person or one's family. Responsibility demands that one leap to the defense, even if the same criticisms framed more dispassionately or from another source normally would have elicited agreement.[29]

Southerners are unwilling to give up on their community or family because of faults and failings. As the writings of Faulkner, Styron, Welty, and others illustrate, good and evil are mixed. One does not overcome evil in society by denouncing that society as a whole, by rejecting it outright. History, of which society is the collective repository, does not leave one because one does not like it. This is the fundamental lesson of Southern literature. It is also the fundamental burden of Southern culture. It can, however, be a strength as well, though too often it has proven a weakness. It has forced silence when outspokenness was necessary, conformity when resistance was demanded, and resistance when accommodation was imperative. It goes a long way, however, toward explaining that while social change in the twentieth-century South was not as simple as might have been desired, it was neither as devastating nor as destructive as some had feared.

Southernness must be understood as a source of identification and socialization. As such it is impossible to escape. As a source of identification and socialization it bears a great deal of responsibility for the behavior and actions of those immersed in it, both good and bad. The problem in the South, and elsewhere, has been the unfortunate identification of the sources of identity with the institutions that bear them. This is an error made as often by historians and sociologists as by members of a society. Fortunately it has been avoided by Southern writers, who have noticed that what is important is the "attitude not the presence of the particular institutions and events that customarily embody the attitude."[30] Unfortunately it has rarely been noted by other white Southerners in the twentieth century, and this failure to separate the truth from its bearers has been the source for most of the conflicts in contemporary Southern history. It goes a long way toward explaining the inability of the dominant institutions in the South, including the Southern Baptist Convention, to respond to the overwhelming challenges experienced by the region between 1930 and 1980.

FOUR

Change and the Southern Baptist Convention

The members of the Southern Baptist Convention never saw themselves as a separate, gathered community. The decision that Baptists would be involved in the world had been made from the beginning. While Southern Baptists might think and act as though they were a righteous remnant viewing the world as an evil and hostile place, they were always in the world, if for no other reason than its salvation.

Baptists overwhelm the other religious denominations in the South; they constitute between 20 and 25 percent of all inhabitants. The sheer size of the denomination mandates that any external changes must involve it and its members. And the nature of change is such that one is compelled to respond to it regardless of one's views about it. Even those sects, religious or otherwise, that choose to reject changes and developments accept the existence of the changes by recognizing that choices must be made. An example is the decision by some to resist the integration of the South's public schools through the formation of segregated academies. The result was the maintenance of the previous system, but the action itself was an admission that the previous system no longer existed.

Some in examining religion in the American South have had exceedingly harsh words for it, and especially for the Southern Baptist Convention. They have claimed that religion in the South has failed in several ways. The first of these is that the denominations in the South have become a "culture-religion."[1] The denominations, especially the Southern Baptist Convention, have been too ready to accept the cultural and political status quo and have failed to challenge the evils in the land. Whether the latter claim is true, and certain evidence suggests that it is not as true as many believe, the former is undoubtedly valid. It tells us too little, however. Religion, and religions, are always immersed in historical and cultural contexts. To say that Southern religion is a cultural religion, while an important sociological claim, is not helpful. One would be hard-pressed to locate a religion that has not been used to affirm the cultural and historical life of its members and society. What most critics mean when they make this suggestion is that religion in the South has not responded to change in the ways they wish it had. This is especially true in terms of race. However, the SBC has not been that far behind most other religious denominations in this regard. This is especially true given its institutional structure. As J. Herbert Gilmore put it, detailing the split over integration at First Baptist Church, Birmingham, Alabama:

> Baptist churches in the South frequently seem to be strongholds of racism. I do not wish to minimize our severe shortcomings or our almost total captivity to the culture, but it is true that the democratic polity of Baptist churches lends itself to washing dirty linen in public. As a result our worst mentality, rather than our best is revealed in the public press. . . . In Christian groups with a hierarchical structure, pronouncements are made by the . . . leaders. Yet at the grass roots level, all denominations suffer equally from the terrible malady of racism.[2]

Many in the denomination admitted that the convention suffered from an unfortunate slowness in responding to issues, regardless of the times or the issues. As early as 1964 Southern Baptist weakness on race was recognized by the convention's Christian Life Commission in its annual report. The report stated, "Our thunderous silence in the face of oppressive injustice for American Negroes has amounted to a serious complicity in the problem." The editor of the *Biblical Recorder* put the same thought this way: "Southern Baptists have very little to brag about, especially in the Deep South states where we are stronger numerically than all other religious groups combined. The responsibility rests heavily on our shoulders."[3]

One may ask what predominantly white denomination in this country responded as well as it should have? What major religious institutions in the history of the world have not been far too close to the sources of power and oppression at some time in their history? This is not to excuse the failures of the Southern Baptist Convention and its leadership. It does suggest, however, that many critics have expected far too much. Institutions will always be limited by their structures and by the humanity of those who inhabit and maintain those structures. A denomination that gave the world Pat Robertson and Lester Maddox also produced Will Campbell, Clarence Jordan, Bill Moyers, and even Jimmy Carter. Did not the religious institution that produced Torquemada also produce Francis of Assisi, and both John XXIII and Pius IX?

That the Southern Baptist Convention did not respond as adequately and as forcefully on the issues as it perhaps should have done is not to say that the convention and its members always resisted change. One should not claim that a religion is captive to its culture until a greater understanding of the culture is obtained and the nature of that relationship has been examined.[4] Cultural interpenetration is a two-way street, and the failings of society with a particular religious structure must be analyzed in light of the possibility that they might have been worse without the religious dimension.

Southern Baptists, both individually and corporately, responded to the changes taking place in the world, the United States, and the South during the half century from 1930 to 1980. There were many reasons for this. The theological and doctrinal commitment of Baptists not to separate from the world has kept them active in events. The world thrust itself upon Southern Baptists, just as it did upon everyone else. Responses had to be formulated.

Many resolutions adopted by the annual meetings of the convention and articles in the various state newspapers have been filled with platitudes and clichés that were not translated into action. This does not weaken the claim that awareness existed and continues to exist. It could be said that Baptist peculiarities have made them less able to implement a great deal of their proclamations into action than other denominations. Yet if all other religious bodies had matched their rhetoric with behavior all evils should have disappeared by now.

On the international level, two issues that interested Southern Baptists were religious persecution and war and peace. The interest in religious persecution stemmed from the historical Southern Baptist witness on behalf of religious freedom for all peoples. In 1928, as the United States was in the process of examining the treaties ending World War I, the convention commended the Senate's refusal to ratify the Lausanne Treaty with Turkey, or any treaty "which does not make provision for and guarantees of the oppressed peoples of Armenia, who have suffered so much injustice and cruelty at the hands of Turkey."[5] The convention also was quick to condemn the elevation of Adolf Hitler to power in Germany and to affirm its support of the Baptist World Alliance's statement condemning Nazi oppression of the Jews.[6] Throughout the 1930s and early 1940s Baptists issued resolutions condemning the destruction of rights and liberties by the armies of Japan, Germany, and Italy.[7]

The resolution on religious liberty approved by the convention in 1939 pointedly noted the problems created by the European dictatorships.

> No issue in modern life is more urgent or more complicated than the relation of organized religion to organized society. The sudden rise of the European dictators to power has changed fundamentally the organic law of the governments through which they exercise sovereignty, and as a result, the institutions of religion are either suppressed or made subservient to the ambitious national programs of these new totalitarian states.[8]

The convention through the activity of the Baptist Joint Committee on Public Affairs also took an active interest in the struggles of Baptists throughout the world. There was a special concern regarding the attempts of various governments to suppress the Baptist witness. The SBC elicited the intervention of the U.S. Department of State when the government of Rumania placed restrictions on its Baptists. This successful intervention was followed by one less so. The SBC attempted to have the Japanese return the property of the Baptist-owned University of Shanghai following occupation of the city. The Japanese, who had transformed the university into a military compound, refused.[9] Even if Southern Baptists had wished to ignore the wider world they could not have done so. The world impinged on them and compelled them to respond, and having the doctrinal ability to respond they did so.

Following the end of the Second World War the Southern Baptist Convention redoubled its interest in ending religious persecution and ensuring that victims of persecutions and violence during the war received fair and equitable assistance. In 1946 the convention petitioned the State Department, requesting that guarantees of religious liberty be included in all treaties of peace. It passed a resolution calling on Congress to amend the Displaced Persons Act "in order to bring to the United States 400,000 such persons in four years" and to remove all "discriminatory clauses hampering the main purpose of the Act." Finally the convention resolved that all forms of religious persecution and tyranny were antithetical to Baptist belief and practice, declaring in 1949 that "communism, fascism, political ecclesiasticism, and anti-Semitism are utterly contrary to the genius of our Baptist concept of freedom and spiritual values."[10]

Events of the postwar world demanded that Southern Baptists continue their concern and activity on behalf of persecuted coreligionists. The victory of the Chinese Communists ended a historic and strong Baptist commitment to China. It also resulted in yet another Baptist martyr. Dr. Bill Wallace, a Baptist medical missionary, was among those teachers of religion who died at the hands of the Chinese Communists. Persecution of Baptists in Spain, Italy, Russia, and Eastern Europe riveted their attention on governmental policy in those countries.[11] Struggles throughout Africa, Asia, and the Middle East also thrust themselves onto the awareness of Baptists. The murder of missionaries in the Congo, Rhodesia, and the Gaza could not but make Southern Baptists aware of strife in the world.[12]

As early as 1956 the Christian Life Commission in its annual report to the convention noted the growing struggles of colonial peoples for freedom.

> The major conflicts of our century are caused by long submerged peoples fighting for their recognition as persons and their inherent freedoms. The major cause for their awakening is the spread of the gospel over the earth. Wherever the Christian gospel has been preached it has awakened in the people a sense of their dignity and worth which has set them straining at the shackles of their bondage.[13]

These movements are seen as positive fruits of the gospel. The Christ who came to free all is indeed active in the living affairs of human beings. While most Southern Baptists probably did not grasp the complexity of the issues involved or the fundamental impact of the movements, the movements were noticed and a positive interpretation was placed on them.

World peace and disarmament were also issues of an international scope that concerned Southern Baptists. In the 1930s Southern Baptists, along with most Americans, still smarted from United States entry into World War I. Many were, therefore, interested in the developments of the international disarmament conference and the Briand-Kellogg Pact. At its annual meetings the convention voted for several resolutions condemning war and warmongering. Among them was one issued in 1940 as war raged in Europe.

> That the continued sacrifice of human treasure and human blood in International war is a wanton and wicked waste for which nations, and particularly their rulers who declare and prosecute war, must give an account to the All Wise and All Just Judge of all the earth.
>
> Because war is contrary to the mind and spirit of Christ, we believe that no war should be identified with the will of Christ. . . .
>
> Our churches should not be made agents of war propaganda or recruiting stations. War thrives on and is perpetuated by hysteria, falsehood, and hate and the church has a solemn responsibility to make sure there is no black out of love

in time of war. When men and nations are going mad with hate it is the duty of Christ's ministers and His churches to declare by spirit, word, and conduct the love of God in all men.[14]

The success of a world court also was in the forefront of Baptist concerns.[15] As early as 1895 Southern Baptists had called on all "governments of the world to resort to arbitration instead of war for the settlement of disputes."[16] The convention had desired the ratification of the Treaty of Versailles, including the formation of the League of Nations, and despite that failure maintained a continuing interest in the World Court and in the possibility of adjudicating international conflicts via some international tribunal. Southern Baptists were involved in the formation of the United Nations; Joseph Martin Dawson carried the petitions of thousands of Baptists demanding that a statement on religious liberty be included in the UN charter to the San Francisco conference.[17] In 1946 the convention's special committee on peace offered six issues that should be addressed by any treaties of peace: 1) no isolationism; 2) democracy—all nations have the right to self-government; 3) an international organization for peace, with the necessary police power and an international court of justice; 4) respect for the worth of every individual, the elimination of race prejudice and habits that undermine respect for the individual; 5) economic opportunity for all people, the elimination of disastrous trade barriers and enforced poverty; and 6) religious liberty, not only tolerated worship but the right to conduct missions, to hold property dedicated to religious uses, to establish schools and printing presses, and to exercise civil rights without discrimination on grounds of religious faith.[18] This latter was a guarantee on which Dawson insisted despite the opposition of the U.S. secretary of state, who felt it would be a stumbling block to the charter's acceptance. The United Nations and its activities were of continuing interest to the SBC throughout this period, and the Christian Life Commission under the authority of the convention maintained a representative at the UN with a status as a nongovernmental observer.

In their interest in international affairs Southern Baptist shared the attitudes of their fellow Southerners. As Alfred Hero has shown, Southerners were much more internationally involved than the rest of the country through the 1940s and into the fifties.[19] Southern senators like Lister Hill, Claude Pepper, and William Fulbright prepared the way for the United Nations and 99 percent of the Southern senators voted to ratify its charter, as opposed to 73 percent of Northern Democrats.[20] Brooks Hays, an influential Baptist layman and president of the Southern Baptist Convention from 1957-1959, also served as a delegate to the UN from the House of Representatives in 1955.

During the 1960s, however, the traditional consensus on war and peace issues began to collapse. Southern Baptists traditionally have attempted to maintain a middle way between pacifism and the condoning of war. Recognizing the fallen nature of humanity and that evil must at times be resisted with violence, Southern Baptists have accepted war as often the only choice for the restraint of evil. In doing this they have attempted to prevent their churches from becoming baptizers of war in the name of the Prince of Peace. Often they have failed in this balancing act, joining many other denominations in that weakness. Rarely, however, has this failure been as great as it was during the Vietnam conflict, when Southern Baptists came far too close to baptizing of the war. In fact, by 1968 twelve of the twenty-nine state conventions had come out in support of American involvement in Vietnam.[21] The SBC itself never completely supported the war, but its demands for a settlement of the conflict always included the catchphrase "honorable peace." It never condemned the war effort, although both the Christian Life Commission and the Baptist Joint Committee opposed it.

The interesting element is not the change in the denomination over peace issues but that the change occurred at that time and over that issue. This must be interpreted in terms of the larger series of conflicts at the time, and the fact that Vietnam itself became a symbol of resistance to (certain) changes or opposition to existing patterns. As late as 1979 conservatives in the midst of attempts to gain control of the denomination were unable to defeat a resolution calling for ratification of SALT II, and in 1978 the convention could pass a resolution calling on "our nation and the other nations of the world to shift funds from nuclear weapons systems to basic human needs, such as education, medicine, and relief from hunger."[22] Internal conflicts were beginning to show, and while they did not necessarily erupt in the area of international affairs they were growing within Southern Baptists' understanding of economics, and on social issues came close to splitting the denomination.

By the 1970s Southern Baptist interest in economics was increasing. Through the activity of the Christian Life Commission the evils inherent in the existing economic system were brought under scrutiny. Simultaneously, however, there was a growing feeling throughout the convention that capitalism was fundamentally the only moral form of economic organization. James Guth in his study of Southern Baptist ministers found that most of

61

them, regardless of their politics, agreed that "the free enterprise system is the only system which is really compatible with Christian beliefs." This strong association of an economic system with Christianity is a surprise to Guth; such "a connection would have baffled saints of earlier ages."[23] Those baffled saints would have included many Southern Baptists.

By living in a culture in which capitalism is a given, most Southern Baptists, along with most Americans, have accepted it as the best economic system although not necessarily a moral imperative. When compared with the functioning, or dysfunctioning, of the economies in other countries, the modified capitalism prevailing in the United States has struck many as much more acceptable and workable. This was especially true in the period following World War II as the economic boom took place. The tremendous growth in consumer goods and disposable income seemed to answer any questions regarding the practical advantages of America's modified capitalism. This general acceptance of capitalism was not formulated as a commitment to it as divinely ordained. "Contrary to the common American view, Christianity is not bound by an iron band to any political or economic system. It has existed in monarchies, city-states, democracies, theocracies, republics, and under slave, feudal, capitalist, and socialist economies."[24]

The pursuit of material possessions always struck the convention and its members as somewhat immoral. The quest for goods seemed at odds with the quest for the spirit. Unlimited capitalism as well as communism were both questionable from this point of view. Both overemphasized the material aspects of human existence by limiting human beings to their economic functions.

For many the economic collapse of 1929 signaled the death knell of unfettered capitalism, a death not to be mourned. The Depression was seen as punishment for the unlimited pursuit of money, a chastisement from God for the failure to turn one's face toward the spiritual. L. L. Gwaltney, editor of the *Alabama Baptist*, was outspoken regarding this.

> Capitalism has made a huge mess of things. In all likelihood there are children now living who will see its complete overthrow.
>   Let it go.
>   Some conservative and modified form of Communism will take its place and the thing which comes will be better than the thing which was and ceased to be.
>   Capitalism, by the help of the government, will readjust itself and doing so will save itself temporarily. But its days are numbered. It may last for a quarter, a half, or a whole century, but some form of socialism is sure to supplant it after a while.[25]

Although Gwaltney was among the more extreme in his views, he was not alone in feeling that the economic policies of the previous decades must be transformed in order to deal with the new imperatives. In a 1935 resolution, the convention recognized the great economic revolution occurring in the United States as well as the

> obligation of governments to function in the matter of social security in behalf of the people. We most sincerely concur in the praiseworthy intention of our government to raise the standard of living of groups of our people and to surround them with those things in life which are designed to culturally and economically make life constructively happy.[26]

The depths of the Depression were not the only moments when Southern Baptists spoke forthrightly of the responsibility of the government to transform economic structures and the need for legal changes to create a more equitable system. In 1978 the convention passed its own Declaration of Human Rights, which called on Southern Baptists churches to be

> boldly involved in championing justice for the oppressed, providing food for the hungry, supporting changes in those laws and systems which abuse the poor while providing loopholes for the rich, doing the things which make for peace, and effecting change where change is needed to support basic human rights.[27]

Southern Baptist interest in economics, however, was not related to systems or policies. Their general approach and understanding was much more scriptural and moral. Possessions were not necessarily bad, but if one had them one had probably gotten them immorally. At the very least they were likely to turn one's mind from God and lead one down the path to destruction. Materialism and goods were an inherent threat to morality and to value.

> In whatever part of the world, however, under whatever system, materialism is mankind's chief foe. Whenever things are in the saddle humanity suffers tragically. Materialism works for the destruction of the whole scale of values. It may mouth that a man is worth a million dollars, referring to the fact that he has managed to get a million dollars, when it is known that he is worth almost nothing to God and his fellow man. The term "making good" has no reference to good. "Standard of living" has nothing to do with standards or living, but describes merely the possession of more things.[28]

This attitude had several sources. One was a general Southern blue-collar attitude toward wealth and privilege that traditionally has been identified with the Northeast and a feeling that political elites fundamentally care little about laboring folk. This attitude was what made the Southern states very supportive of the New Deal and was behind the statement one cotton mill worker made to an anti-New Deal reporter that "Roosevelt is the only man we ever had in the White House who would understand that my boss is a sonofabitch."[29] The more spiritual nature of this attitude was put most eloquently by Southern novelist Marion Montgomery.

> Whether laws for the control of nature are advocated by the industrial right, or the industrial left, those laws are derived from the same principles. The blueprints of laissez-faire capitalism or state socialism, or the totalitarian amalgam of the two in communism, are strikingly similar when the controlling vision has lost sight of the relation between nature and nature's God. But if man's final end is the consumption of goods, whatever the mechanism advocated, the "quality of life" thus championed must inevitably be determined at the level of a merely biological function.[30]

This spiritual attitude has been that generally shared by Southern Baptists. Materialism, which is the code word for capitalism run rampant, is as evil and as ungodly as "atheistic communism." The overemphasis on material goods and the greed that leads one to ignore God and to engage in immoral activities is a constant concern. The condemnation of such behaviors is phrased in scriptural and biblical terms.

Sunday school lessons examining Amos could easily use the scriptural texts as indictments of the gross immorality and personal depravity resulting from too much wealth. As one lesson writer stated, Amos argued primarily against cities, exchange, and the concentration of money in the hands of a merchant and ruling class. This accumulation of both people and money is destructive of values and gives rise to the feeling that one can do anything. "Having more ready wealth, men and women are the more tempted to invest it in luxuries of questionable value."[31] An adult Sunday school lesson put the entire attitude toward wealth succinctly in a statement regarding the story of Zacheus. "He was rich, and riches tend to dull the edge of spiritual concern."[32] Finally a writer put the relationship between communism and materialism into a comparative perspective.

Much of the world is dominated by either communism or materialism. Both are attempts to build a society without God. In our country the influence of materialism is so strong that the distinctions between right and wrong are blurred. There is unconcern for morality in high and humble places. Even though there is in our land the largest church membership in our history—about 63% of the population—there is also the highest crime rate in our history.[33]

It is obvious that Southern Baptists historically have not had a vested interest in the existence of capitalism, although there was a general cultural acceptance of it. As far as Southern Baptists have been concerned there existed no scriptural basis for capitalism, just as there existed no scriptural opposition to it. The struggles of the past two decades, however, have begun to alter this traditional understanding of economics. There are three main reasons for this, only two of which are germane to the discussion. The other reason, however, is important and must be kept in mind. This is the opposition to communism and the propagandizing in favor of free enterprise that dominated much of the 1950s and 1960s. The increased equation of free enterprise with the United States and its use as an element in the struggle against communism could not fail to have an impact on the country as a whole and especially on a group opposed to communism on religious grounds.

More important, however, was the increasing affiliation of opposition to capitalism with those whose opinions on social and other issues were antithetical to Baptist beliefs. Baptists as individuals exhibited a common tendency to adopt positions previously unheld in order to continue to be in opposition to those they oppose on social issues. The continuing impact of the civil rights struggle played its part in this. White Southerners, and one must assume many Southern Baptists as well, have had difficulty isolating their attitudes on race from their economic attitudes. Not only have some white Southerners allowed their racial feelings to determine their economic beliefs, they have allowed their racial attitudes to cause them to act against their own perceived economic self-interest.[34]

Finally there is the emphasis of unfettered capitalism as one plank of the political program of the religious right, the politically conservative Fundamentalists. Here it is possible that the opposite event transpires. Agreement on certain theological, social, and moral issues could lead one to adopt attitudes held by those with whom one agrees. This, combined with the organizational strength of the Fundamentalists, goes far in explaining the general transformation of the attitudes of some Southern Baptists on economics. This linkage helped to turn views of economics from a relatively amorphous rejection of any system as scriptural and an emphasis on the evils of the accumulation of wealth toward a positive view of capitalism or free enterprise as more in line with the moral demands of the Christian life. While the Fundamentalists have had some affect on the attitude of Southern Baptists regarding economics, they have profited more from the peculiar alignment of issues than from any direct actions on their part. Their greatest impact on the convention has been in the area of social and political issues, as the members have attempted to deal with changes in morals.

The radical transformation of sexual values from the 1950s on had a tremendous impact on Southern Baptists. This was heightened by the media glorification in the more extreme examples, as well as a general outspokenness. All of this caused Southern Baptists to feel they were losing their ability to rear their children in the manner they saw fit. This fear, as well as manipulation of it by those with a set political agenda, caused many a tempest in a teapot.

The Christian Life Commission organized a seminar entitled "Toward Authentic Morality for Modern Man." Among the speakers, including professors from the convention's seminaries, were Anson Mount (at that time public affairs manager of *Playboy*), Dr. Joseph Fletcher, and Representative Julian Bond. The seminar was conceived as an opportunity to confront and seriously deal with the issues of the day. While the presence of Joseph Fletcher, author of *Situation Ethics*, was sufficiently bad, the presence of Anson Mount was enough to give many apoplexy. Most critics managed to keep the debate centered on the issue of authentic morality, of which many felt there was only one kind, that is Christian morality, no debate being necessary. The "filth," as one writer put it, published in *Playboy* did not meet that criterion, nor did Dr. Fletcher's situation ethics with its claim "that there are times when it is better to lie, steal and commit adultery and fornication than not to."[35] At times, however, the final straw was the presence of Julian Bond, the "Negro state legislator in Georgia" who "is a leftist out to destroy America."[36] Many did not to see any need for such a seminar. The claims advanced by Dr. Hudson Baggett, editor of *The Alabama Baptist*, that "We need to understand the heavy pressures and subtle temptations inflicted upon the Christian as he seeks to live his faith in today's world," had little effect on those for whom morality was God-given and therefore inherently unchangeable.

Unless it would only strengthen the faith of the Christian and help him to see that Christ alone is his strength and bulwark against temptations of this or any other age. Christians can understand what God is saying to them about morality in 1970 because it is no different to what he has said since He first began talking to man. Rejection of God in Adam's day is still rejection of God today. Murder today is no different than the day Cain slew his brother. Adultery the day Moses received the law on Sinai is still adultery today.[37]

Although they looked askance at many of the changes taking place, Southern Baptists did not pretend they did not exist. They attempted to respond to those changes and to direct them. Their entrance into the sex education field is representative.

In 1969 the convention passed its first resolution on sex education, directing its Christian Life Commission to take the lead in producing sex education materials for use by the denomination.[38] During the same year the debate over the seminar on authentic morality occurred, the training union manuals for intermediate pupils (thirteen to sixteen years old) introduced the topic of sex education and attempted to deal with sexuality honestly yet within the moral structure of theology and doctrine.[39]

The lessons themselves were neither particularly descriptive nor prurient. Some felt, nevertheless, that they were out of line. They believed the attempt itself was unnecessary, for "this world will never be helped by what we do for today's society or how well we teach our children sex education." Such activities were not part of the responsibility of the churches, which should "teach the Word of God, letting our young people know that *without* Jesus there is no hope now or ever."[40] Others, including several of the teenagers for whom the lessons were written, felt differently. In fact many of them manifested a sensitivity and awareness that should have shamed their elders. As one fourteen-year-old put it:

Today's young people face many decisions about many things, among these is the question "What does God expect of me as a sexual being, and what does the Bible say about sex?" I only wish the T.U. lessons were more thorough, because most parents do not know how to answer this question.

In closing I have two requests to make of parents. First of all pray for the young people of your church and elsewhere as they face many decisions about life in general. Secondly ask a young person how he feels about the lessons about sex.[41]

67

Another letter came to the *Alabama Baptist* from an entire Training Union class. In this letter the children criticized the seamy side of sexuality shown in movies, books, and on TV. The whispered conversation of other teenagers, and even well-meaning people who do not want sex to be discussed, give the impression that it must be dirty. They felt that these lessons gave them a greater understanding of themselves as sexual beings as well as the ability to deal with their normal sexual desires. They were thankful that they were being "led to have Christian attitudes toward it."[42]

Several adults tied the need for such lessons to changes in society, such as increased mobility, two-paycheck families, and the breakdown of parental control. These writers felt that the slack had to be taken in somewhere, and where better than in the church.[43] The church not only can, but should, minister to the needs of the contemporary world. This did not mean that the world should dictate the beliefs of the church, but the answers given by the church should be to the questions of the modern world. Their opponents, of course, saw the issue from the opposite position. They felt that the same answers applied to all questions. They failed to realize that the problems to which Christianity must respond change, even if Christ remains the same yesterday, today, and tomorrow. On the latter both sides agreed: the answers must be scriptural and morally conservative. Some maintained a staunch opposition to dialogue with today's world. Others felt that the church must respond to the world as it is, while still remaining the church.

The general response of the convention, however, was that the church should respond to the world by disagreeing with it. On the issue of sexuality the church did indeed have a legitimate ministry to human needs as well as an obligation to challenge and chastise the ways of the world. As a 1977 convention resolution put it, the churches should:

> speak out against this permissiveness of the new morality and, under the leadership of pastors and parents, supplement and reinforce the sex education taught in the home in order to strengthen the biblical teachings of marriage and fidelity to the marriage vows.[44]

That the convention and most of its members rejected a permissive sexual ethic should not imply an opposition to sexuality. The convention insisted on a scripturally based ethic that condemned the misuse of sexuality as a sin. It recognized that God created sexuality for human enrichment, communication, and procreation. God calls humans to a celebration of their sexuality. God as

68

redeemer provides the means by which humans can express their sexuality in a responsible manner. God calls on them to express love and to work to provide responsible teaching about sexuality.[45] What emerges is a willingness to admit that change is indeed occurring and that the church is somehow responsible for dealing with that change, of moving it in directions that are consistent with the will and law of God. In terms of changing sexual morality we find an awareness by the convention that pressures and demands on people are changing and that the church must respond to these new demands, not that the new demands are acceptable. The church must stand against the world, for the world. It must make the gospel message speak to the world as it is, not conform to the world.

Here one begins to understand why there are few self-identified Southern Baptist liberals. For Southern Baptists "liberal" has connotations of theology and morality that predominate over the political use of the term. Thus, even politically liberal Southern Baptists identify themselves as moderates or conservatives. This has produced complications in attempts to deal with the onslaught of a politically conservative Fundamentalism in the 1970s and 1980s.

The Southern Baptist Convention had battled with the Fundamentalists fifty years previously and had managed to keep the body within its traditional limits.[46] This resurgent Fundamentalism of the 1970s had a new organizational strength and political agenda.[47] It managed to combine a theological conservatism congenial to most Baptists with a manipulation of the fears and hostilities engendered by the times to create a potent political and religious force. Most of the Fundamentalists in the SBC, however, have not had a strong institutional affiliation with the body. Guth highlights this in his study of political activism among Southern Baptist ministers. The attitudes of the minsters he studied reflect the divided nature of the convention. When asked to respond to the activities of such organizations as Moral Majority the ministers split down the middle, with 3 percent claiming membership, 43 percent generally approving, and 47 percent expressing general disapproval of the activities of the organization.[48] Those ministers who self-identified as Fundamentalists and who fell along the most conservative line in terms of political policy were also those who were "somewhat marginal to the organizational life of the denomination, predominating among pastors who have never attended a Southern Baptist Convention and among those who have served only briefly in their current position."[49] The influence of the Fundamentalists has been strongest in the areas of doctrine and the position

69

of the convention on social issues. It is in and through this arena that they will continue to have their greatest success, for reasons directly linked with the SBC's history.

Members of the Southern Baptist Convention are a fairly conservative group theologically and socially. Opposition to alcohol, tobacco, and gambling have constituted a part of their mission since the mid-1880s. Personal morality, honesty, the sanctity of marriage, and responsibility have dominated in their teachings on ethics and their codes of behavior. Long before liberals discovered it, Baptists were concerned about violence in movies and on television. They also worried about the impact both technologies would have on family and community. The problems of urbanization and wealth (materialism) also have vexed Southern Baptists. They knew the problems with cities long before sociologists pointed them out. Baptists knew this not only because they were Southerners and shared the typical Southern view of cities as immoral and inhuman; they knew it because it was scriptural.[50]

Holding such views, Southern Baptists watched the radical transformations in the American social landscape with alarm. The urbanization, increase in wealth and materialism, growth in licentiousness, and breakdown of parental authority all cut close to the beliefs they held as individuals, Southerners, and Baptists. The struggles they had previously undertaken to keep their counties dry now turned into fights against drugs with strange names. The morals of society changed, allowing activities once hidden. Some demanded that such behaviors be granted acceptability and legitimacy. Some even suggested that they were right. This was more than many could bear. Race riots, crime, rampant sexuality, drugs, and violence struck far too hard at a people already undergoing extreme social and political dislocation. Fear gave way to anger. This was not only the righteous anger of Jesus clearing the Temple, it also was the anger of the Southern white who had been pushed too far once too often. Wilbur J. Cash claimed that in every Southerner "was the boast, voiced or not . . . that he would knock hell [heck, for Baptists] out of whoever dared to cross him." It was just this feeling that accounted for much in the Southern character. Cash credited it with the behavior of the Confederate soldier.

> [T]he thing that sent him swinging up the slope at Gettysburg on that celebrated, gallant afternoon was before all else . . . nothing more or less than this conviction, the conviction of every farmer among what was essentially only a band of farmers, that nothing living could cross him and get away with it.[51]

Southern Baptists, like many in America from the 1960s on, began to feel that the world had gone permanently out of kilter. Everyone's opinions and values became important except for theirs. Changes in traditional moral values along with overwhelming social and political dislocation caused a great deal of fear. Fear gave way to anger and resentment. This resentment partially explains the failure of attempts to change the denomination's name; that was at least one thing they could hold onto. Fundamentalists manipulated this anger and resentment in their pursuit to further their political program. This was especially true in terms of social issues. A large part of the Fundamentalists' program consisted of efforts to strengthen what they called traditional moral values. This primarily consisted of attempts to roll back those changes in society that had taken place during the 1960s and 1970s by attacking the legal developments that had made them possible. Abortion, homosexuality, pornography, premarital and extramarital sex, and sex and violence in the media all became targets of their activities.

The traditional conservative doctrinal and moral positions of Southern Baptists have made them sensitive to the arguments of Fundamentalists. As William O. Carver put it discussing an earlier struggle with Fundamentalism in the convention, "Being all but unanimously conservative, and loyal to the historical and scriptural fundamentals of Christianity Southern Baptists make an inviting field for capital 'F' (fundamentalist) agitators."[52] On certain issues there was a fusion of interests, although traditional Baptist reticence to affiliate with non-Baptist bodies has made this fusion difficult to actuate. By examining the positions of Fundamentalists and the so-called Christian right one can see how their insistence on conservative theology and social conservatism could translate into an acceptance of other parts of their political program.

The attempts by Fundamentalists to gain control of the denomination are reflected in the transformation of the convention's position on social issues. This suggests how the location of political ideas and theology could transform an institution's position on other issues. The acceptance of your position by your enemy can lead you to adopt the opposing position even if that position had not previously been natural to you. This could be summed up as the ideological version of the "the enemy of my enemy is my friend" style of politics. You begin to identify what you are for in terms of what your enemies oppose.

In 1973 the Supreme Court handed down its decision in *Roe v. Wade*. The Court ruled that the state had no compelling reason to limit abortions, at least during the first trimester of pregnancy.[53] From the beginning many religious groups—not only Protestant Fundamentalists but Roman Catholics and Orthodox Jews as well—objected to this ruling. Southern Baptists, however, did not react quite so strongly. From 1971 to 1979 the messengers to the Southern Baptist Convention basically passed the same resolution on abortion.[54] The statement was consistent with traditional Baptist thinking and understanding both theologically and doctrinally.

The convention affirmed a historically held biblical view of the sanctity of human life, called abortion a serious moral and spiritual issue, and declared that Christians have a responsibility to deal with all moral and spiritual issues that affect society. The resolution declared that "the practice of abortion for selfish nontherapeutic reasons wantonly destroys fetal life, dulls our society's moral sensibility, and leads to a cheapening of all human life." It affirmed the convention's commitment to the biblical sacredness and dignity of all human life, and rejected any indiscriminate use of abortion, calling upon all to work for a "change in those attitudes and conditions which encourage many people to turn to abortion as a means of birth control." Finally, however, the resolution reaffirmed Baptists' "conviction of the limited role of government in dealing with matters relating to abortion" and supported "the right of expectant mothers to the full range of medical services and personal counseling for the preservation of life and health." Not only did the convention refuse to call for a constitutional amendment overturning the court's decision, it affirmed the limited right of the government to involve itself in the issue.[55]

Between 1974 and 1980 the convention continuously rejected attempts to add a statement in favor of a constitutional amendment, although in 1976 a rider was attached rejecting as contrary to Southern Baptist doctrine and tradition the suggestion that "Southern Baptists should become activists in support of permissive legislation." In 1980, however, in the midst of attempts by Fundamentalists to gain control of the convention, a resolution was passed calling for appropriate legislation to prohibit abortion except to save life of the mother.[56] There appears to be a strong correlation between the increase in the strength of Fundamentalists and the transformation of the convention's position on abortion.

Issues like abortion present a particularly complicated series of questions for Baptists. They force Baptists to choose between two goods within their value system, a belief in the sanctity of human life and a commitment to soul competency and human freedom. The earlier Southern Baptist pronouncements on abortion carefully balanced these two attitudes. They found a way to condemn abortion because of what it does to the human being and to human society and at the same time to affirm, indeed proclaim, that it is an issue with which the government has little to do. To accept the Fundamentalist position on abortion Baptists had to subsume their traditional attitude toward freedom. This they did in 1980 by accepting the demand of Fundamentalists calling for legislation to limit abortion. Yet the Fundamentalists still could not carry the day, as the convention also rejected any legal attempts to nullify the decision of the Supreme Court on school prayer.[57]

Another element separating Southern Baptists from full-scale participation in Fundamentalism was the difference in issues they considered important. The Fundamentalist obsession with homosexuality is well known. While Southern Baptists are critical of homosexuality as a sin recorded in the Bible, they have not manifested an obsession over the issue. Their statements rejecting homosexuality are tempered with the recognition that all persons can be saved "from the penalty and power of sin through our Lord Jesus Christ, whatever their present individual life style."[58] In fact an examination of the convention annuals, newspapers, as well as survey research among ministers and members shows a greater concern about alcohol than homosexuality.[59]

Southern Baptists as a whole also have not had the same theological concerns as the majority of Fundamentalists. Fundamentalist insistence on premillennialism—if not dispensationalism—and biblical inerrancy and their scholastic theology have separated them from historical Baptist thought and doctrine. As one Southern Baptist writer put it:

> Fundamentalists have a basic misunderstanding of the nature of the Christian life and the character of Biblical literature. For the vital experience of personal faith in Jesus Christ, fundamentalism has often substituted intellectual acceptance of the doctrine of his deity, undergirded by a series of rational proofs. For a body of Holy Scripture which is interwoven with the saving acts of God in history, fundamentalists have substituted a static book of doctrine and precepts, which is liable to all kinds of arrangements according to dispensational schemes, eschatological charts, and creedal "tests of fellowship."[60]

The struggle over the influence and impact of Fundamentalism has managed to polarize the SBC and move it in contrary directions. At the time when the denomination had become more outspoken on social issues, a newer, politically conservative movement began to develop as well. A great deal of the growth of the conservative wing must be attributed to its manipulation of hostility resulting from social upheavals and changes of the recent past. The growth of the more activist element in the denomination must be attributed to those changes as well.

Changes in morality, social structure, and technology transformed society during the twentieth century. The SBC is still struggling with responses.

Changes in all those areas, however, are dwarfed by the radical transformations in race relations and church-state separation. These two issues riveted Southern Baptists more than any other denomination. Struggles over responses to them created those tensions in the denomination which have resulted in the polarization and conflicts of the present day.

FIVE

Race and Southern Baptists

When change in the twentieth-century South is considered, race is that issue which most often first comes to mind. This occurs with good reason. If racial behavior was not the greatest single arena of change in the past fifty years, it was the most visible and emotional. White supremacy, segregation, the "Negro Problem" were major elements of life in the Southern United States until the last fifth of this century. Some have considered race the defining theme of the South. While this is an exaggeration, the formation and organization of the segregated South demanded energy and initiative that could have been expended with better result elsewhere.

The structures and forms of segregation have been discussed above. Several points should be stressed. The first is the impact the presence of the black population had on white Southerners. As Cash put it, "the Negro entered into the white man as profoundly as the white man entered into the Negro—subtly influencing every gesture, every word, every emotion and idea, every attitude." Ralph Ellison also saw this impact: "southern whites cannot walk, talk, sing, conceive of laws or justice, think of sex, love, the family or freedom without responding to the presence of Negroes."[1]

Equally important was the impact the black underclass had on the mental life of nonelite white Southerners. This underclass provided whites with a social status that could not be taken away regardless of how far they descended on the social scale. What Cash has said about slavery is equally true for postemancipation white supremacy.

[It] elevated this common white to a position of say the Doric Knight of Ancient Sparta. Not only was he not exploited directly, he was himself made by extension a member of the dominant class—was lodged solidly on a tremendous superiority . . . he could never publicly lose. Come what may he would always be a white man. And before that vast and capacious distinction, all others were foreshortened, dwarfed, and all but obliterated.[2]

The only difference was that to a great extent poor whites were exploited directly, because of their position vis-à-vis blacks. Regardless of the difficulty of the job or the lowliness of the wages, it could always be given to a black at even less money. The psychological security provided by the structures of white supremacy had a negative counterpart in the economic insecurity resulting from the existence of an institutionalized underclass. Here certain of the complexities in the structures of white supremacy can be seen. Southern blacks were a fulcrum upon which a great deal of activity moved. Like a fulcrum, however, their responses and actions were basically inert, or at least perceived as such. Blacks were a tool used by whites for their own purposes. For the economic and social elites they functioned as a means for keeping nonelites in line. The memory of Reconstruction served a similar purpose for achieving political control and the solidity of the Democratic Party. The threat of the collapse of white supremacy served to prevent fundamental challenges to the existing structures.[3] For nonelites white supremacy served as a source of social and psychological security. It gave poor whites a place in the social hierarchy that they could never lose, as long as they continued to observe the articles of white supremacy.

Stating it this way, however, makes it seem more intentional than it was. The structures of white supremacy and segregation resulted from historical becoming. They were responses to issues and events. With their implementation they took on lives of their own, and beyond the original reasons could be manipulated to serve the interests of different groups and bodies. As white supremacy became increasingly entrenched in the psychological and social structures of the region it also became the touchstone that affected every idea and every policy that struck the region. From woman suffrage to federal aid to education, segregation reared its head. Would the passage of the Nineteenth Amendment give black women the vote? Would the money given to education by the federal government bring with it the end of segregated schools? White supremacy became a procrustean bed in which all actions and policies were forced to lie. Even if the policy or the law was not the least bit related to the issue those opposed to it could, and did, find ways to intrude white supremacy. To confuse any issue one opposed by bringing up segregation was a dominant theme in Southern politics in this period, and if that were insufficient the threat of another Reconstruction and a "Force Bill" could be added as well.[4]

This should not give the impression that nothing other than maintaining the racial status quo dominated Southern thinking. It was an element of the world always present. It was latent in the society and could be drawn upon anytime to serve various interests. Usually, however, its existence was preconscious. It was a given, organizing human behaviors and attitudes from birth. For most it was the way things were. While elements of it might seem at times odd and strange, it surrounded one growing up in the South with the appearance of a seamless garment. Like air, it became noticeable only when absent. Many stories could illustrate this, but perhaps the best, because it is so simple, is that of Harry Leland Mitchell, a dry cleaner from Tyronza, Arkansas.

Mitchell, one of the founders of the Southern Tenant Farmers Union, was attending the Continental Congress for Economic Reconstruction—organized under the auspices of the Socialist Party, the railroad unions, and the National Farmer's Union. Beyond the usual speeches and drafting of resolutions was a demonstration led by Norman Thomas against the Cairo Hotel for refusing to let rooms to the New York delegation, which included several blacks, among them A. Philip Randolph. Mitchell remarked later, "It had never occurred to me that it was wrong. Negroes had their place, and we had ours."[5] If one already involved in thinking and acting contrary to accepted opinions could fail to question the structures of segregation on his own, why not more so those people less actively critical of their world?

It is important to distinguish between an active racism, a deep personal animosity toward people of another race, and a structural racism where one is blind to the racist elements surrounding one. There exists also a passive racism in which one accepts the inferiority of a people. This inferiority is not seen as innate but results from a lack of cultural and educational advantages. Given time they will someday catch up, yet now must be restrained and guided. In feeling this, however, one may have no animosity or hatred for those people. In fact one may dedicate one's life to their uplift. Still the racism remains.

Most, if not all, Southern Baptists, like most Americans and indeed most people, were guilty of the second form of racism, the acceptance of the structures that retain a group of people in an inferior state solely because of their racial background. A majority were guilty equally of the third. Some undoubtedly were guilty of the first, yet they were not a majority and inside the denomination had little impact. Most Southern Baptists could not understand the issues involved in the civil rights struggles. Even fewer could understand the black power movement. Suddenly it seemed that their accepted modes of believing, their inherited world, were under attack. They were called evil, and yet they had *done* nothing. They had not created the system, and felt that they personally had nothing to do with racism. They did not hate blacks, and in fact had lived with them all of their lives. Real racism, in their minds, existed in the North. Certainly many Southerners would have agreed that relationships between the races were not perfect and that more should have been done "to help our black brothers and sisters."[6] Such change, however, takes time, and is no place for the Federal government to intrude with force. If those northerners who came South to help the blacks truly had any concern for them they would have stayed in Chicago, New York, Boston, and Los Angeles and served them there. Instead, many Southerners believed, they came South for personal political reasons, not out of any interest in the welfare of blacks.

What of Southern Baptists in this regard? What was their position, their history regarding race relations in the South? The history itself is long and varied, with several twists and turns. Originally most Baptists in the South had rejected black chattel slavery as inconsistent with the word of God, a position that did not endear them to their neighbors. How should they then respond to slaveowners desiring church membership? For some the solution was simply to refuse them fellowship and to remove from fellowship those who came into possession of slaves through purchase or inheritance. There are, however, problems involved with this solution. If the state government forbids the manumission of slaves, is it possible to require a congregant to disobey the law? The issue is further clouded by the fact that even if one did manumit slaves in violation of the law, the manumission was invalid and those slaves would be resold. Would it not be better for those godly men to retain their slaves instead of putting them at risk to the highest bidder?

Involved as well was the issue of evangelization. The hostility of Baptists and Methodists to slavery was more than sufficient reason for slaveowners to forbid them access to their slaves for the purposes of preaching and evangelizing, thus condemning themselves and their slaves to damnation due to the unreasonable attitudes of the Baptists and Methodists. Baptists would bear the responsibility for this, and if the important element were the salvation of souls their response ought to be more flexible.[7]

Finally, as always, social and political events were involved. The continued threat of slave revolts made any opposition to slavery suspect, especially after the Denmark Vesey and Nat Turner uprisings of 1822 and 1831. The growth of Baptists in the South and the passage of time put more of the membership into positions where owning slaves was not only a possibility but a necessity befitting their station and the size of their landholdings. The local churches as free and independent bodies could overturn any threat of disfellowship by a majority vote, an occurrence that became increasingly probable as the body attracted more and more members capable of being slaveholders. The passage of time also increased the number of members whose socialization into a slaveholding culture made them see it less and less as a moral evil. As a result there was increasing interest over whether slavery was a moral issue. If one considered slavery solely a political issue that the state was empowered to control, slaveholding itself ceased to be a moral issue. The moral issue became that of treatment of slaves and the moral duties incumbent upon the slaveholder. Slavery then could be seen as morally neutral, its morality dependent on one's behavior as a slaveholder and toward one's slaves.

At this point slaveholding as an institution ceases to be of interest to the church and rests in the hands of the political authorities. The conflict that led to the formation of the Southern Baptist Convention becomes more understandable as a result. Northern abolitionists in the general convention were making what had become, for most Baptists in the South, a political issue into a moral one. By doing so they were violating the spiritual nature of the church.

This is a complex and serious issue. The main issue involving race relations between 1930 and 1980 is segregation. One way of discussing segregation is to declare it inherently immoral and inequitable. Or one can decide that it is morally neutral, its morality or immorality depending on the mode of implementation. That is to say, it is a political and legal entity—like the speed limit—and in itself has few if any moral ramifications. The moral issues revolve around one's responses toward those of other races on an individual personal level, how one treats others as sisters and brothers in Christ, not necessarily on how one votes. Here the dominant position in the Southern Baptist tradition differs from the arguments for apartheid put forward by the Reformed church in South Africa. There separation of the races is seen as religious imperative, while within the SBC the majority of members saw it as neutral and one could be for or against it without one's salvation or morality coming into question. As late as 1972 the Sunday School Board could call for "a climate that assumes those who disagree about race are nevertheless sincerely seeking the Christian position."[8] Or as one newspaper editor put it:

> This paper has never defended segregation of the races, nor has it defended the unreasonable attitude of some persons about it, but it does defend the right of the individual to hold an opinion on the subject without being unchristianized by those who hold an opposite view.[9]

There were, of course, Southern Baptists who felt that segregation was a violation of Christian principles. But the issue could be placed in the realm of the worldly, outside the arena of the church. Just because segregation might be regarded as acceptable is not to say that all forms of prejudice were considered so. Christian living was to determine one's relations to all human beings. Segregation did not abrogate one's responsibility to follow the biblical injunction of love toward one's neighbor. Segregation was solely a political construct, approved by the highest court in the land,[10] and as such had no impact on the obligation of one person toward another. Interpersonal relationships, not political structures, were dictated by the Christian law of love.

What, however, were the responses of members of the SBC and the convention itself to the series of events breaking down the walls of white supremacy in the American South? As they were on most issues, their responses were disparate and varied, yet there seems to be a discernible ground base. There is a studious commitment to following the law, avoiding violence, and responding to all people in the manner of Christian love. Billy Graham's plea in 1960 is representative of this. He called on all to obey antisegregation laws and to go out of their way "to be courteous, kind, and gracious to those of the other race on a personal basis."[11] This is a common theme in many official and editorial pronouncements. Here the inherent conservatism of the body is observable. While not taking the lead in bringing about social and political change, it also had no use for violence and chaos. Instead the various commissions of the convention took it upon themselves to educate the membership into the necessary changes. This happened quite often in the face of hostility and resistance by segments of the membership, yet this hostility was mediated by acceptance of those same positions by other segments of the membership. One sees a great deal of this give-and-take in the pages of the weekly state Baptist newspapers.

These issues need to be enlarged upon. The remainder of the chapter analyzes the responses of Southern Baptists and the SBC to three issues. The first is the struggle of its membership to deal with changes in the racial status quo in terms of two systems of socialization. These are the belief system of Southern Baptists as Christians who feel themselves bound by the law of love for neighbor and their position as white Southerners living in a particular historical moment socialized into the values and mores of that position. They chose their world no more than other people. Like everyone else they had to deal with their inherited traditions. To perceive possible alternatives would have required them to reject their world and the world of their parents and grandparents. There are inherent conflicts between the Christian law of love and the folkways and legal structures of racial segregation and white supremacy.

This chapter also illuminates the magnitude of plurality within the denomination. The documents show tremendous diversity and disagreement over the changes and questions of the period.

Finally there is the constant conflict between sociopolitical action and the work of evangelization. To what extent does one take precedence over the other? For Baptists the answer is easy. Evangelization is the preeminent purpose of Christians. This complicates the issues of the time. It is easy to use evangelization as a smokescreen for one's reluctance to challenge social and political structures. Because it is possible for it to be used that way, however, is no reason to assume that every time the claim is made it serves such a purpose.

Human beings find themselves members of different groups and organizations. Some they are born into, some they choose, others choose them. People are introduced into the values, beliefs, and activities of those groups; they are socialized into membership. For some groups, like the society into which one is born, the ways of being a member are preexistent and preformed. The society precedes individuals.

From the beginning it imprints itself upon them. White Southerners in the first three-quarters of this century found themselves members of several societies that gave them particular advantages and that carried sets of values, beliefs, and codes of behavior. The first of these was their status as citizens of the United States. They were Americans. This conferred a certain status on them. It inculcated in them traditions and beliefs, those things we see as distinctly American. They were Southerners, with all the ramifications of that designation and world. They were also white in a society where a person's race was determinative for the possibilities and activities of one's life. To be white was to be privileged, and was to secure those privileges at the expense of those who were not.

Southern Baptists were, however, also Christians operating simultaneously under another set of demands and values. This conflict between the privileged nature of white Southerners and the Christian demand of love for neighbor is summed up succinctly in a young people's Sunday school lesson.

There are barriers between people erected by custom and sometimes sustained by law. Sometimes we enjoy the benefits of being a member of a privileged class or race, and contribute our part toward maintaining the barriers. But in the light of his attitude toward Samaritans we are forced to the conclusion that Jesus has already condemned such customs and distinctions.[12]

The problem of implementing such demands without limiting the ability of the body to evangelize remains. On the most cynical and tawdry level, like anyone selling a product Baptists were rather unwilling to antagonize potential customers. The same attitude may be put in a more positive light, by considering that by alienating a person from the Christian message one puts that person in risk of eternal damnation. Such a risk is exceedingly great. It is also unnecessary. If conversion of the human person is the activity of God, and it is impossible for people to change themselves as a result of the fall, then changes and improvements in social and political structures can come about only through converted individuals. In order to change racial attitudes and abolish hatred, the first step must be the conversion of the individual. Conversion is not only more important than the transformation of social and political structures, it is a prerequisite for such transformation. Certainly the church must be interested in the formation of laws and policies in accord with Christian principles, but that is not its main purpose.

This is discussed more fully later. The preeminent issue here is the conflict between the dual sources of socialization. While the Supreme Court's decision in *Brown v. Board of Education* was not the first major racial issue of this period (agitation over federal antilynching legislation holds that position), it was the first in a series of federal and judicial actions that brought about the end of legal segregation. When the Supreme Court handed down its unanimous decision in 1954 responses in the Southern Baptist press and in the convention were restrained and supportive.

The decision was . . . almost inevitable in the light of Christian truth, the claims of democracy, and the demands of the world situation.[13]

Whether we like it or not it is now the law of the land, a fact which we must face and adjust ourselves to as good citizens and loyal Americans.

No problem is ever settled until it is settled right. Dodging, evading, or seeking to sidestep this issue is no settlement at all. Calling names and impugning the motives of the Supreme Court is puerile. It is now imperative and incumbent upon Negroes and whites alike to cooperate in calm clear thinking and courageous action in the interest of saving our free public school system.[14]

The convention itself took a firm stand on the decision, which was issued shortly before its annual meeting in June. The Christian Life Commission, the denomination's social issues committee, presented a recommendation applauding the decision and calling upon Baptists to assist in its implementation. The recommendation called the decision "in harmony with the constitutional guarantee of equal freedom to all citizens and with Christian principles of equal justice and love for all men."[15]

The descriptions of the decision as consistent with Christian truth and equal justice and love for all presuppose an understanding of the imperatives of the Christian law of love. In order to understand how that operated for Southern Baptists it is necessary to show how they have interpreted it in terms of relations between the races.

Even during the period in which they were resisting the abolitionists and setting a course for separation, Southern Baptists never rejected the idea of the humanity of blacks or of their equality before God. They struggled to convert slaves, and they allowed blacks to preach, to act as the instruments for conversion not only of blacks but also of whites.

Certainly the feeling that blacks were inferior in cultural terms, sadly lacking in the amenities of Christian civilization, was strong. This does not abrogate the fact, however, that Baptists felt a moral demand to respond to blacks even in their slavery as sisters and brothers in Christ. The willingness to accept slavery was not the same as a willingness to justify it, as Donald Mathews has illustrated.

> Southern clergymen were still embarrassed to defend servitude, lacing their letters, columns, and books almost ritualistically with such phrases as "I am no advocate for *slavery*," or "The Bible does not by any means *Justify* slavery. It only serves to explain African slavery in this country." And the ritual, for all its self-delusion, moral obtuseness, and mindless repetition betrayed an inner agitation and persistent moral "cramp" which made more than one evangelical slaveholder damn "the curse of slavery!" and hope against hope that something could be done to fight it and its consequences: "the grossness, the prejudices, the littleness, the selfishness which taints to corruption the atmosphere of public life" in the South.[16]

The similarity between this statement and Carson McCullers's claim regarding the effects of white supremacy on white Southerners in the twentieth century are worth noting. McCullers claimed that *The Heart Is a Lonely Hunter*, while descriptive of the individual human condition, was especially applicable to the situation of white Southerners because of the constant nagging pressure applied by the awareness of participation in a great wrong.

> There is a special guilt in us, a seeking for something had and lost. It is a consciousness of guilt not fully knowable, or communicable. Southerners are the more lonely and spiritually estranged, I think, because we have lived so long in an artificial social system that we insisted was natural and right and just—when all along we knew it wasn't.
> The fact we bolstered it with laws and developed a secular liturgy and sacraments for it is evidence of how little we believed our own deceits.[17]

This moral itch constantly nagging at Southerners, telling them that somehow the existing conditions were wrong and unjust, was felt keenly by evangelicals. Baptists were not the least of those affected. From 1930 to 1980 the struggles to accommodate the demands of Christianity and the given structures of Southern society led to reasonings and subterfuges nearly as convoluted as those of the nineteenth century.

For providing a ground of feeling in the convention at the beginning of the period the report on interracial relations issued by the Southern Baptist social committee in 1933 is superb. The report, written by Arthur Barton, is succinct and valuable. Our common humanity is proclaimed and buttressed with scripture: "The unity and solidarity of the human family as the creation of God is clearly set forth in God's word. (Acts 17:23-28)." This common humanity is not only physical as "corroborated by all the facts of biology, psychology, and human experience," but also spiritual and moral. Christ died for all. This reality puts an obligation on whites. At this point Barton takes an interesting and disjunctive turn. Instead of making this obligation the typical white responsibility for black uplift he straightforwardly challenges white thinking by demanding that whites cease thinking of blacks as instruments in their hands.

> We must cease thinking of Negroes primarily in terms of our own convenience, as a race divinely doomed to perpetual servitude to the white man's will. In the teachings of Christ every human being is endowed with all of the high and sacred functions of humanity and no human being is to be regarded as a mere means to some other's end.[18]

Here is a strong biblical case for the equality of races, an important element given the centrality of the Bible in Southern Baptist thought. Also the human sciences are offered as corroboration. This is an interesting, though not uncommon, move. At this time the Scopes trial was a memory less than nine years old and evangelical resistance to evolution was based nearly as much on its perceived threat to the concept of common humanity as to the biblical view of creation.[19]

Around this time the internal conflicts begin operating on a more immediate level. In 1932 and 1933 agitation over the famous Scottsboro case was strong. The Supreme Court overturned the conviction in 1932 and ordered a new trial. The *Alabama Baptist* applauded the decision, and the editor of the *Biblical Recorder* confessed shame and humiliation regarding the case, especially that the prosecutor made appeals to prejudice in order to attain conviction and that no Alabama attorney could be found to take the case. In a later article the editor mentioned his hope that prejudice could be avoided at the next trial, but doubted this would be the case as long as the defense attorney tried to force the prosecutor to "call a colored witness Mr."[20]

This is an interesting point, regardless of whether it was made, because such a move was seen as a tactical error, or because the editor who honestly desired justice to be attained was unable to see beyond his upbringing in a world where that was not done. If the former, it shows him concerned for the welfare of the black suspects. If the latter, it illustrates how the competing forms of socialization created the responses of Southern Baptists to their world. Even the perception of it as a tactical error showed tremendous sensitivity to the world in which the trial occurred and the pressures placed on those who lived in that world.

It is this combination of factors that is interesting: the relationship between the world the Southern Baptists inhabited and to a great extent created, the American South, and their religious world. For Southern Baptists there remained a great deal of flexibility and responsibility for Christian action within the limits of a segregated South. Whereas the structures of segregation were quite often seen as improper if not wrong, there were few if any frontal attacks on them. Southern and Baptist personalism is at work here. Attitudes and judgments controlling actions are directed at the individual and emerge from the individual. Thus Southerners are capable of directing animosity and distrust toward corporate groups yet manifest less of that animosity toward individuals than do other sections of the country.[21] The editor of the *Baptist Standard* summed up the reasons for this. Commenting on a B'nai B'rith report on historical Christian anti-Semitism the editor admits the validity of the historical claims, acknowledging that many wrongs have been perpetrated in the name of Christianity. Such occurrences have been the result of the union between church and state, and he respectfully requests that Baptists be exonerated due to their nonconforming status and the fact that the personal judgment of individuals by merit is the sole criterion used by Baptists in their dealings with others.[22]

The command incumbent upon the individual to respond within the realm of the Christian law of love is constantly and consistently reiterated throughout all the conflicts over the changes in the South's racial barriers.

> There are many things happening and threatening which do not meet with the approval of many, but it will behoove all of us to live within the law.
> We must admit that hatred has no place in a Christian's life. Love is the driving force of a Christian's actions, and if we will follow the way Christ has set forth for us, all things will definitely work together for good to us all.[23]

With the passage of the fair housing act in 1968 a similar call went out. Baptists were urged to initiate contacts and become acquainted with blacks in order that a greater understanding could take place. Such actions, it was thought, would alleviate fears and help calm potential shock and overreaction.[24] There existed not only an overwhelming feeling that the actions of individuals toward others were important, but also a feeling that events would take place quickly. There was a naive belief that changes in legal structures would have an immediate impact on the familiar world, transforming it instantly. One, therefore, should be prepared for them.

This personal dimension, however, was not the only element at work. There were those who saw that regardless of one's behavior toward the other, structures could preclude the establishment of justice and equality. This point often was made in the Sunday school and Training Union lessons. "Anyone, for example, might be a close friend of a person of another race but at the same time help maintain a system built upon the conviction that people of that race are inferior."[25] Such articles, however, seem to be directed primarily at youths and children. Adult lessons were less likely to undertake controversial issues. This is an important and illustration of the denomination's role as educator. The lessons also show the denomination's felt responsibility toward the South and its particular problems: "No one in the first century, for example, could foresee the problems of our economic order, or of the relationships between Negroes and white people in the South, or of modern warfare."[26]

Southern Baptists were not, however, only Baptist Christians socialized into that particular world. They were also Southerners, white Southerners, who inherited a set of beliefs and values. Their responses were affected by those beliefs and values. The fusion of Baptist and Southern personalism is an example already seen. There are others. The South and Southerners have seen themselves often as embattled, hated, and misunderstood by the world at large. This mentality goes far toward explaining Southerners' feelings of difference, their regional identity. In the conflicts over the dismantling of legal segregation this feeling arose again. Southern Baptist responses often reflected this Southern feeling of embattledness, even in the midst of granting the validity of claims for justice. Such an occurrence was seen in the discussion of the Scottsboro case. There are many others like it.

> There is a warmth between the races in the South which is not found anywhere else in our nation. This warmth must continue and because of this evidence of personal regard for each other, we must make it known that we are not against anybody and see to it that this warm relationship continues. We believe, because of this warm relationship, the South will solve its problems much faster and better than other areas.
>
> We realize that many people throughout the nation, and especially in the South, have been harassed and invaded by people from other sections of the country who have grave problems they need to solve themselves before they seek to take the mote out of other people's eyes.[27]

These quotes appear in articles calling for obedience to secular laws and responding in the manner demanded by the Christian law of love. Still there operates the issue of the embattled South undergoing a reinvasion by people determined to destroy it. The quotes, however, are only a moderate version of this attitude, and perhaps it is important to see the more extreme position.

When George Wallace became governor of Alabama in 1963 he was committed to resisting attempts by the federal government to integrate the state's schools. His campaign had been based on his opposition to integration and the need for resistance. Although Wallace was a Methodist, the invocation at his inaugural was delivered by a Baptist minister, Dr. Henry Lyon. Its symbolic meanings could in no way be lost on its audience.

> Almighty God, Father of our Lord and Saviour Jesus Christ, we thank Thee for this glorious occasion which brings us to this sacred place, the Cradle of the Confederacy—where in the yesterdays, our ancestors dedicated themselves to the cause of States Rights and freedom for the souls of men.

87

> We beseech Thee for strength as sons and daughters of the sovereign state of Alabama that we may pledge anew our allegiance to the flag of the United States of America. Fill our souls with unflinching courage as we join hand and heart with all friends of democracy to preserve the Constitution of our great nation. May we rather die than surrender this God-given heritage.[28]

Here there is a fusion of particularly Southern symbolic elements: "the Cradle of the Confederacy," ancestors, sovereign state, state's rights, "preserve the Constitution." It is a view of the South as once again embattled, the lone soldier standing up for the right, for constitutional government. It is not a simple inaugural prayer asking God to direct the new governor. It is just as much a declaration of war as was Wallace's inaugural address. It is a call to martyrdom just as strong as anything issued in John Bunyan's England. But it is much more Southern than it is Baptist, even though it was a call from one Baptist to others. More important, it was issued by an influential figure at an important event. It had an impact, just as much as Wallace's proclamation of "Segregation today, segregation tomorrow, segregation forever." Only two months before, however, the Alabama Baptist Convention had passed a resolution calling on elected officials to provide "constructive leadership." Simultaneously they pledged their "cooperation and support to those in authority, when such leadership is given, refraining at all times and under all circumstances and conditions from any act of violence or demonstrations of prejudice or hatred against anyone."[29]

The messages formulated and articulated by elites were mixed. There existed much variation and difference over the issues. Much of this conflict played itself out in the pages of the state newspapers. Every position found its counterpoint. The diversity and plurality emerged from all classes and all sections. This plurality becomes important for examining how the membership was divided over the issues at hand, issues of such magnitude and importance that they easily could have rent the institution. Yet they did not.

While white supremacy in Southern society was a given, there were countervailing values. Some of these were of a religious nature, others were of a liberal democratic stripe. Unfortunately they were more than matched by those of a racist and intolerant nature. The competing and struggling visions found their way into the literature. The person who perhaps best characterizes the opposition to racism from a Baptist and Southern source is Will Campbell.[30]

Campbell's understanding of our common humanity from a Christocentric position is deeply rooted in the Baptist tradition. It is also exceedingly sin-

convinced, as summed up by his statement that, "We are all bastards but God loves us anyway."[31] While his way of putting it would offend most Baptists, even those who agree with the sentiment, it is a view fundamentally rooted in the gospel law of love, and Paul's command to "Be ye reconciled one to another." This is an important point. Campbell's compelling understanding of human sin is much more congenial to Southern Baptist thinking, and to the Southern theological tradition, than would be a more humanistic and theologically liberal position. For Campbell, God loves us in spite of the sin and depravity common to us all. Even the most degenerate and disallowed of the world have something to impart to those most perceived as worthwhile by the church and the world. While few Baptists, and few other people, would be willing to follow Campbell in his application of this view to everyone from black sharecroppers to Ku Kluxers, from prisoners to music stars, it has strong roots in Baptist thought due to their self-perception as outsiders. In Campbell's thinking there exists the element of the Southerner as estranged. This combines strong biblical and religious claims couched in a Southern vernacular with an emphasis on personalism. These are joined with his distrust and dislike of institutions, which he understands as instruments designed to divide human beings, not to bring them together. The government, the church—all institutions—tend toward separating those inside from those outside. The same is true for laws. Even laws designed to overcome separation and hatred at best only control external behavior. They do not, cannot, alter human attitudes and thinking. Like laws requiring religious observance they make people hypocrites and idolaters. They ignore the fact that true reconciliation, like true belief, comes only through the actions of God upon the individual through the death and resurrection of Christ. Because the crucifixion reconciled humanity to God, people may now be reconciled one to another, but only through human contact and the Christian law of love as a result of the creating, redeeming, and sustaining power of God.

Baptist opposition to segregation finds its home among all types and groups of peoples. Certainly it might be more common among the better educated and those more financially secure—those who know they have different opportunities and choices—but it is not confined to them.

One way of handling this issue is to examine responses to particular issues in the political and social realm. Baptists were confronted with the demands for integration of their colleges, hospitals, and churches. It is possible to examine how these events transpired and were brought about. Some occurred with little fanfare; others generated a great deal of tension and animosity.

Certain churches integrated quietly as early as 1962, especially in Texas and Oklahoma. Other attempts at integration resulted in conflict and division. Such was the case of First Baptist Church in Birmingham where attempts to integrate the church resulted in the resignation of the pastor and youth director who favored it. Three hundred members also walked out of the church and joined the pastor in forming a new integrated congregation.[32] Examining the issues in such a topical way, however, is not the most productive method. Many of the most illuminating events were in-house conflicts and unnoticed by the wider world.

One of the most interesting involved the conflicts over a set of texts used in home mission and foreign mission study courses. They were designed to integrate the Christian message with the tremendous social changes the world and the South were undergoing. These books—*A Tide Comes In, Bulldozer Revolution*, and *Trumpets in Dixie*—were the source of much controversy and conflict.

Most of the criticisms of the books centered on the claimed absence of scriptural background and their inattention to spiritual issues. Some felt that these had been sacrificed to propaganda and modernism; many felt that the writers lacked spiritual teaching and knowledge. People occasionally allowed their anger to overcome them, and the issues became more related to the times. This was undoubtedly the case with one woman who, responding to a claim in one of the books, wrote, "I do not feel like a Negro who or anyone else who washed my car would be in need of me washing his feet . . . I do not feel we should meet with Negroes socially, at public functions, or in our Southern Baptist Conventions."[33] But such opinions were not allowed to go unchallenged. A most direct and open statement was written in response to criticisms of these books.

Dear Dr. Baggett:

Having a limited education I have hesitated to write this letter, but my convictions are strong and I am going to say what I want to in the best way I know how.

I am writing concerning the letter in the March 7th edition of the *Alabama Baptist* paper from the First Baptist Church, Silverhill, Ala. The only literature mentioned in that letter I am familiar with is "Africa—Arrows to Atoms" and "Trumpets in Dixie." Dr. Baggett, I found nothing in those two books objectionable and non-scriptural. The only way that I can understand anyone objecting to them in any way is to have a deep rooted racial prejudice. God made different colored people so I'm sure He loves each of us equally. It is a shame when we have had to let the law do for our colored people what Christian love should have done long ago—only we should have done much more. I am distressed to see the letters continue to appear in the editorial column that reek with racial prejudice. . . .

May God forgive us all and fill our hearts with love for all mankind.[34]

This letter was not an anomaly. There were always objections made to editorials, articles, or letters that challenged the legitimacy of integration. Simultaneously there were articles and editorials that engendered these letters. Leon Macon, who edited the *Alabama Baptist* from 1954 to 1968, had strong feelings on the issues. He may not have been a virulent racist, but he was definitely a segregationist. He also strongly resented the intrusion of outsiders into the South in order to straighten out its racial problems when there were an equal number of problems in the North. "Those who came into Alabama and created these disturbances came from areas of the country where there is more racial violence than in the south."[35]

Macon was active among those Deep South clergymen who worked to weaken the convention's pronouncements on race. This applied not only to the statement drafted for the 1964 meeting, which was a major critique of racism in all its forms and of resistance to integration, but also of the statement issued by the Executive Committee after the bombing of the Sixteenth Street Baptist Church in Birmingham in 1963. Charles Trentham had submitted a resolution deploring that occurrence. This resolution was opposed by Macon and the other representatives from Alabama who, while deploring the bombing, felt that it was wrong to point "to one area as the point of guilt and neglect the over-all picture." That would make it appear that "we endorsed the rapes, stabbings, church burnings, and violence in other places and thus make Birmingham appear to be the only guilty city."[36]

While this reasoning borders on the ridiculous, the interesting element is the list of crimes and sources of violence. Bombings and church burnings at this time were crimes primarily tied to whites; the inclusion of rapes and stabbings, crimes primarily attributed to blacks in the Southern mind, illustrates Macon's constant insistence that the sources of racial violence were not limited to whites.

Macon, however, continuously published articles in disagreement with his views and there were always letters challenging him. One of his constant bugbears was the issue of forced social integration, another monster used to frighten Southerners who might forget their cultural reality. In formulation it goes something like this: If the federal government can force integration in schools, in transportation, in restaurants, and in housing, why can it not force me to integrate my friendships and my social life?

Combined with this was the fear that the intermingling of the races at school and elsewhere would inevitably result in intermarriage and the "mongrelization" of the races. This too was a fear of Macon's, and one he was not loath to raise. He did it, however, by raising the issue of Jews and their resistance to intermarriage and God's commandment to them not to intermarry. He attempted to use this to show that one could be in favor of integration and opposed to intermarriage. The issue then became scriptural and more complex. Yet there were those who were willing to tackle even this most delicate question and challenge his rejection of intermarriage.

Mrs. Creed Gilbreath wrote a provoking letter in response to Macon's article. She pointed out that Jewish opposition to intermarriage rested on the issue of faith and religion, not race. Baptists also want their children to marry others of their faith, for as Paul writes in II Corinthians 6:14, "Be ye not unequally yoked together with unbelievers: for what fellowship hath righteousness with unrighteous?" She followed with what for the time was a most outspoken claim: "The color of one's skin has nothing to do with what he believes, so a Negro could marry a white person of the same faith and what sin has been committed? I think none." She then challenged the very possibility of discrimination coexisting with Christianity.

> Discrimination is the natural thing for human beings, but Christians are to live on a higher plane than just doing the natural thing. We would have no trouble with this problem at all if every Christian would practice this command of Jesus: "Therefore all things whatsoever ye would that men should do to you, do you even so to them" (Matt. 7:12).[37]

Even the claim that the South's racial problems were caused by outside agitators met with resistance and argumentation. A man identifying himself as a deacon of the Sylacauga Baptist Church and a native Alabaman wrote to reject Macon's claim that "our race problems are caused by outsiders." At most, he wrote, these outsiders have brought to the surface "conditions that have existed since the Negro was first brought to the South as a slave. These 'agitators' have served only to inform the Southern Negro that he is a human being, he is an American citizen and as such is entitled to the rights that are available to any citizen."[38]

I certainly do not claim that the people who wrote these letters represented the views of most of the people in the South at that time. What is important is that these opinions existed, that people gave voice to them, and that they found their places in a denominational publication. Another interesting fact is that opposition to integration, with perhaps one exception, was never formulated on the basis of religion. Opposition to segregation was almost inevitably so formed. Even a conservative minister like W. A. Criswell went on record claiming that "I don't think that segregation could have been or was at any time intelligently, seriously supported by the Bible."[39] Those opposed to integration inevitably couched their opposition in terms of it being not the purpose of the convention to involve itself with such issues; there were other issues that should take precedence. Some of these were formulated very carefully.

> We believe that much of the racial tension in the South today is due to provocations by political-minded people of the Northern part of our country. While they apparently stir up trouble in one section of the country their homeland is racked by violence, crime and the same identical situation they are trying to solve in our midst. We do not believe we should drag our church into this political issue, but remain faithful to the law and to the principles of Christ.[40]

Others were formulated neither so carefully nor so diplomatically. An example is a men's Sunday school class that complained about finding the same sort of brainwashing regarding the "integration of the races" in The *Alabama Baptist* that they had become accustomed to getting from "the Federal Government and all types of news media." They found this offensive and stated that it was their wish and prayer "that you continue to publish the works and acts of God, and leave the mixing of the races alone."[41] Here is an obvious use of the doctrine of the spiritual nature of the church to avoid dealing with a compelling social problem. The refusal to deal with it is to ensure its continued existence. But there were other sides to this as well, such as the sincere belief that an overcommitment to the issues engaging the world would steadily weaken the evangelical mission of the church.

An argument often raised in favor of this view was the consistent decrease in membership of those churches engaged in the ecumenical movement and that expended their energy on social and political questions. While it had been an issue among Southern Baptists since the formation of the Federal Council of Churches it became more heated and controversial as the complex issues of race, poverty, the Vietnam conflict, and sexuality began to dominate the news. The rise in crime and criminal behavior, the breakdown of social organization and control—all this bore the markings of a world separated from God, and separating itself farther. It seemed that efforts to apply the teachings of Christ to social conditions had "been a miserable failure. Crime in our age has reached an all time high." This criminality and immorality consisted not only of robbery and murder but included "deceptive corruption inside our government and business world."

> We think it is time the churches cease trying to compromise their convictions by uniting physically and begin to preach Jesus Christ and him crucified, to a lost world. . . . Any accomplishments made by the Uniters have shown no spiritually moral fruits and these things alone should cause this group and the liberals among us to realize that Christ is the answer and we have no authority to preach about His teachings except through Him.[42]

This did not imply that the gospel rejected working toward social improvement, only that "the primary emphasis was not placed upon this in the scriptures." It is of the utmost importance that people "get as excited over people being saved and knowing God's will for man's soul as they are for reformation here on this earth."[43] But there was growing concern that decreasing interest in the work of the spirit had weakened the world's ability to deal with sin and evil. The growth of the churches had not been matched with a concomitant growth in the Kingdom of God. "It is easy to recognize the reason why, for so many denominations are emphasizing the social gospel alone, forgetting that people must have the spirit of obedience which comes through the New Birth."[44]

The struggle over the appropriate response to the changes in the legal and social structures of white supremacy caused difficulties for Southern Baptists and for the Southern Baptist Convention. It also resulted in many contradictory responses. In the same year that W. A. Criswell, a leading Southern Baptist conservative, declared the rejection of black members by individual congregations "manifest hypocrisy," the Sunday School Board withheld an issue of the youth magazine *Becoming*, fearing that its racial content would antagonize some members.[45]

The denomination's struggle to determine the correct manner of response to the competing views and conflicting demands of its membership is best seen in the statement of the Sunday School Board issued in 1972. It called for "a climate that assumed that those who disagree about race are nevertheless seeking the Christian position."[46]

Throughout the 1970s the passions aroused by the racial struggles became muted. In 1974 the convention elected its first black vice president and an increasing number of predominantly black congregations requested affiliation with the convention.

The growing spirit of anticolonialism in Africa and Asia became a challenge to racism. The existence of white supremacy was constantly raised as a detriment to world evangelization. While many tried to make the point that missionaries should explain that they represented no governmental body or legal structure but only the Kingdom of God and the universal Christian fellowship, the disjunction between what was preached in Guinea and practiced in Georgia was too great to ignore.[47] Missionaries pleaded with the convention and its membership not to be sent to win the colored peoples of the world and then have their hands tied by events at home. "Half-page pictures splashed on newspapers around the world of white men's dogs being set on Negroes embarrass us and set the course of Christ back a decade each time it occurs."[48]

Also what was known as foreign missions in this country was not mentioned by that name in other countries. Southern Baptists were having to deal with a new world and a new set of realities throughout that world. Some resisted that responsibility, feeling that all of these changes were going against the will of God and the demands of Christianity. Others felt that the demands of Christ inhered within those movements and that it was the duty of a Christian to respond in a scriptural and prayerful way. It was the time to throw off the shackles of outmoded traditions and respond to new realities, at least insofar as that was scripturally possible. As an immensely complex institution the convention began to feel the effects of its divisions and its diversity. As Bill Leonard has seen, the issues of the recent decades left their impact on the Southern Baptist Convention. These conflicts broke down traditional cultural and denominational restraints and resulted in "tensions long present in Southern Baptist life [becoming] more pronounced."[49] The social and political changes of the past several decades did not cause these internal denominational conflicts, but they brought to the surface the inherent diversity and complexity of the denomination.

In the Southern states this complexity manifested itself most visibly over the issue of race and the changes in the racial status quo. While that issue has moved from a boil to a simmer in recent years, other issues have arisen to replace it. The biggest of these is the debate over the relationship between organized religion and the state.

Issues of church and state traditionally have exercised Baptists more than most other denominations. Baptists have constantly and consistently been on the side of religious liberty and the separation of church and state. In the late 1970s, however, increasing numbers of Baptists began to retreat from that historical position. By the early 1980s several came out in favor of the school prayer amendment as well as other positions historically anathema. These newer conflicts were still related to the old sources and changes, issues involving interpretation of scripture, the nature of the denomination, and the social changes experienced by the nation and the South in the recent past.

While most Baptists, both individually and corporately, continued to resist state encroachment into the religious sphere, this new element became increasingly stronger. The period from 1950 to 1980 saw many new problems and questions emerge in this arena.

SIX

Southern Baptists and Church-State Relations

The struggle for religious liberty and church-state separation always has been a Baptist struggle and an important defining characteristic. Other religious bodies shared in the struggle, but in the fight for religious freedom for others, as well as themselves, few can match the Baptists' effort and intensity. Baptists were influential in creating the form that church-state separation took in this country. Their efforts were commended by such noted thinkers and politicians as Benjamin Franklin, Thomas Jefferson, and James Madison. While Baptists have never had the notoriety that attended groups such as the Quakers, the number of Baptist "martyrs" is not insignificant. In the mind of the thoughtful Baptist the existence of these martyrs has always been associated with the union of the state and religion, or attempts by the state to control religious thought and behavior. This is as true of Soviet persecution of Russian Baptists as of seventeenth-century England, which saw the imprisonment of such Baptist notables as Thomas Helwys, who died therein, and John Bunyan.

From 1930 to 1980 the issues involving the separation of church and state became more complicated. One reason for this was the increased activity of the federal government. The need to deal with the problems raised by the Depression, the Cold War, and systemic poverty moved the government into new arenas, arenas that often strained the boundaries between religion and government. These new issues required new rules, and the judicial system increasingly became the arbiter of what was acceptable. New decisions had to be made in order to keep up with the new realities. Alongside the demand for the courts to adjudicate for the new realities was the increased application of the Fourteenth Amendment. This brought into the federal judicial system cases from the state systems.

These events forced Baptists to find their voice on the issues of religious liberty in a way that had been lacking since the early nineteenth century when they had been involved in the struggles to remove the last vestiges of a state-supported church in Massachusetts.

This is not to say that they had turned their backs on their heritage for a hundred years, but only that the issues had not been paramount in the nineteenth century. During that period slavery and the Civil War had taken precedence. The events of the twentieth century gave rise to tremendous struggles over religious liberty. To a great extent Baptists, and especially Southern Baptists given their numerical and financial strength, were dominant in these struggles. Before launching into a discussion of the events from 1930 to 1980, a closer examination of the sources of Baptist actions on behalf of religious liberty is necessary.

The historical Baptist positions on religious liberty were brought to England's New World colonies by British Baptists. There they were expanded and refined. As in England, colonial Baptists were a weak minority. Many of the colonies perceived them as troublemakers and sowers of dissension. This was especially true in Massachusetts, which sought to create a new form of the ordered society under God, and Virginia, where the re-creation of the Old World was the goal. The presence of Baptists threatened those attempts. The threat did not come from Baptist desires to overthrow the civil society, but from their view of humanity's relationship to God and their way of being in the world. Their attitudes fundamentally challenged the premises on which the sociopolitical structures of Virginia and Massachusetts were based.[1]

John Leland was an able and creative early American formulator of the Baptist position on the relationship between religion and the civil realm. He was involved in the struggle for the guarantee of religious liberty in the Constitution and in the states of Virginia, Connecticut, and Massachusetts. Leland also was involved in the American South throughout much of his career.

Leland's positions on the relationship between religion and the political order are grounded in fundamental Baptist theology. The source of these premises is the individual's ultimate and sole accountability to God for her or his beliefs. No intermediary can perform that duty for the individual, not state, priest, or parent. Therefore, none has the right to bind the conscience of the individual, for the individual must be free to act in the manner he or she considers most acceptable to God.

98

Every man must give an account of himself to God, and therefore every man ought to be at liberty to serve God in that way that he can best reconcile it to his conscience. If government can answer for individuals at the day of judgement, let men be controlled by it in religious matters, otherwise let men be free.[2]

Leland also based his arguments for the freedom of the individual's conscience on scripture. Not only was one as an individual answerable only to God but attempts to enforce uniformity of belief either by the state or by a church were unscriptural and violated the bases of the Christian religion.

Had a system of religion been essential to salvation, or even to the happiness of the saints, would not Jesus, who was faithful in all his house, have left us one? If he has, it is accessible to all. If he has not, why should a man be called a heretick because he cannot believe what he cannot believe, though he believes the Bible with all his heart? Confessions of faith often check any further pursuit after truth, confine the mind into a particular way of reasoning, and give rise to frequent separations.[3]

Leland did not, however, base his opposition to enforced religion solely on religious grounds. Many of his arguments were those of an Enlightenment thinker. Just as Baptists dealt with a dual socialization in their struggle over the issues of race, they had another system of dual socialization operating on the issue of religious liberty. Here the two sources worked together. Since Baptists had the fortune of rising alongside the development of liberal-democratic institutions, they were freed from the burden carried by those denominations whose traditions viewed church and state working in tandem. Baptists like Leland and deists like Thomas Jefferson could find a fusion of interests on the issue of religious liberty as well as constitutional government. Whereas many have seen this fusion resulting from radically different sources—the one fearing the prostitution of the church, the other of the civil realm—both rejected any attempt to coerce the thinking of the individual. Leland and Jefferson had comparable views of the duties of government. This shared understanding of the worth of the individual and of the freedom of the individual conscience made the political union of Baptists and deists in late eighteenth- and early nineteenth-century America more than a marriage of convenience.

Government has no more to do with the religious opinions of men than it has with the principles of mathematics. Let every man speak freely without fear—maintain the principles that he believes—worship according to his own faith, either one God, three Gods, no God, or twenty Gods; and let the government protect him in so doing, i.e., see that he meets with no personal abuse or loss of property for his religious opinions.[4]

This statement could as easily have been written by Thomas Jefferson, politician and deist, as by John Leland, Baptist minister. Both felt that the duty of the government was to protect its citizens from one another. The fundamental law, the Constitution, was to protect the citizens from the government and to provide an arena in which competing views could struggle in order that truth might win out. To Leland's mind, as to Jefferson's, truth needed no assistance from the state, and error deserved none.[5] For this reason Baptists traditionally have rejected opening the public purse to support religion. Leland put it most adequately when he stated that

> if government says I must pay somebody, it must next describe that somebody, his doctrine and place of abode. That a moment a minister is so fixed as to receive a stipend by legal force, that moment he ceases to be gospel ambassador and becomes a minister of state.[6]

Baptists extended this thinking to all the forms of applying government funds to, or through, religious bodies. For the most scrupulous, like Leland, it even applied to the paying of military chaplains by the government. For most it extended to the funneling of relief funds through organizations affiliated with particular denominational bodies. This Baptist scrupulosity has made them look exceedingly peculiar to other religious bodies whose tradition of affiliation with the state caused them to see nothing wrong about the two working hand in glove.

The expansion of the role of the federal government in the twentieth century, however, gave rise to new and more complex issues. As programs involving federal funds increased, the boundaries of separation became exceedingly vague. Through this period Baptists managed to maintain their historic position on church-state separation. Because historical and theological sources existed to draw from, Baptists were well equipped to respond to these issues. Their activity in this realm provides a striking counterpart to their inactivity on civil rights.

Baptists were not limited to historical sources in their struggles to define and maintain religious liberty. It was a constant issue for them and its importance was framed in such articles as the Memphis Confession of Faith in 1925 and reiterated in the Kansas City Confession of 1963. The convention regularly reaffirmed its historical position on religious liberty, and maintained an ongoing interest in issues involving religious liberty. Perhaps the most important document on religious liberty issued by the convention in our period was the "Pronouncement on Religious Liberty" of 1939, which became the source for the "American Baptist Bill of Rights" issued later that year.[7] This document set out the sources that drew Baptists to the conclusion that religious liberty and the freedom of conscience are the manner set forth by God in the New Testament for the organization of religious life.

The pronouncement began by stating the fundamental acceptance of the worth of the individual. It is to this individual that the work of the gospel is directed by example, by preaching, and by personal testimony. Every individual soul has the right and ability to deal with God and God's demands without the need for an intermediary. Any attempt to deny anyone the "right of direct access to God is to usurp the prerogatives of the individual and the function of God." The church is a body composed of regenerate believers and is not to be identified with any particular denomination or group. The church is a body without formal organization and cannot, therefore, enter into any contractual relations with the state. Baptists reject the union of church and state for these reasons and denounce any special privileges to any denomination, especially those that may seem to offer state approbation of a particular body or its ecclesiastical structure. Baptists understand that they are citizens of two commonwealths and that in all things not contrary to the spirit of God are to obey the powers that be, not from wrath but from conscience. As the freedom of conscience is an inalienable gift from God it cannot be given up, and since the absolute freedom of conscience is not only for oneself but also for one's neighbor it must be constantly defended.[8]

Between 1930 and 1980 several issues arose against which the doctrine of church-state separation needed defending. The most important involved the transfer of governmental monies to denominationally affiliated institutions. (Examples are federal aid to parochial schools, to hospitals, and colleges run by religious bodies.) Also the propriety of funneling relief money through church-affiliated institutions became a topic of conflict. Other events included the appointment of a United States ambassador to the Vatican, the presidential candidacy of John Kennedy, and the increased number of church-state cases heard by the Supreme Court. Southern Baptists also maintained a continued interest in issues of religious liberty throughout the world, both in the denomination and through their membership in the Baptist World Alliance.

The formation of the Baptist Joint Committee on Public Affairs is a watershed in the Southern Baptist struggle for religious liberty. The Southern Baptist Convention formed its Committee on Public Relations in 1936 by expanding the mandate of its committee on chaplains. The Northern Baptist Convention and the National Baptist Convention, USA, followed suit by forming their own committees in 1937 and 1939 respectively. In 1941 they officially merged to form the Joint Conference Committee. In 1939, before their official merger, they issued a joint statement on religious liberty approved by all three conventions, their "American Baptist Bill of Rights." This document ended with the following statement:

> Believing religious liberty to be not only an inalienable human right, but indispensable to human welfare, a Baptist must exercise himself in the maintenance of absolute religious liberty for his Jewish neighbor, his Catholic neighbor, his Protestant neighbor, and for everybody else. Profoundly convinced that any deprivation of this right is a wrong to be challenged, Baptists condemn every form of compulsion in religion or restraint of the free consideration of the claims of religion.
> We stand for a civil state, "with full liberty in religious concernments."[9]

The early years of the committee saw a concern with those issues that would form, to a great extent, the agenda of the committee and of the Baptist conventions in general. They opposed Roosevelt's attempt to appoint Myron C. Taylor as his personal representative to the Holy See with ambassadorial rank.

Baptists also opposed Roosevelt's attempts to provide federal subsidies to parochial schools. In fact the chairman of the Baptist Joint Committee, E. Hilton Jackson, argued the losing side in *Everson v. Board of Education*. In this case the Supreme Court ruled that it was within the police powers of the state to provide transportation for children attending parochial schools.[10] This would not be the last case with an involvement of the Baptist Joint Committee and eventually more cases would be won than lost. Baptist opposition to governmental assistance to private schools was not limited to direct transfer of monies, but included equally such indirect transfers as the provision of transportation and textbooks by the various states. The opposition to any governmental aid to church-related schools was absolute.[11]

While Baptists steadfastly remained true to their rejection of monies from governments, the increased activities of all forms of government in this period, especially the federal government, made the issues increasingly complicated. It became more difficult to determine what really constituted a violation of church-state separation.

Some of the earliest issues of church-state separation and the increased activity of the federal government involved measures adopted to deal with the Depression. These ranged from the use of relief workers to improve the buildings and grounds of churches to the provision for religious worship in towns built and administered by the Resettlement Administration.[12] In between were issues involving National Youth Administration funds to students attending denominational colleges, the application of Social Security to ministers and employees of religious institutions, and providing Federal Housing Administration loans to churches for repairs.

Questions about relief funds arose later during the War on Poverty when Baptists challenged the legality of allowing church-related organizations to administer poverty programs. Instead they urged that all such programs be run by the state and federal governments.[13] The principle also involved foreign aid. Baptists opposed the federal government's use of religious organizations to disburse goods and monies overseas. Education funds allocated under Kennedy's Alliance for Progress also came under scrutiny, as a result of their administration by the Roman Catholic church in various South American countries.[14]

Two major events will be examined in detail to illustrate the responses of Southern Baptists to the new realities. The first is the issue of governmental aid to sectarian schools, particularly the passage of the Higher Education Facilities Act of 1963. The second involves the decisions of the Supreme Court regarding government-sponsored prayer and Bible reading in public schools. Both of these share a similar time frame, and draw out illustrative points regarding Baptist opposition to any attack on religious liberty.

Baptists have from the beginning opposed federal aid to denominational schools, including not only direct aid but also such hidden aid as would be given through the various voucher plans supported by people such as Milton Friedman and William Bennet, secretary of education during the Reagan administration.[15] Baptists have never opposed the existence of religious schools, only the use of public monies for their maintenance and support. From this, some people have deduced that they are thereby anti-Catholic, a leap of logic that strains the imagination. While one could not claim that none harboring anti-Catholic feelings hid behind the cloak of religious liberty, the most important reasons for the conflicts were radically different understandings of the relationships among the individual, the church, and society.

Coming out of a continental model of the state, the Roman Catholic church was accustomed to controlling its own elementary and secondary schools and to receiving government support in maintaining them. Believing that secular education was a misnomer and that all education should be tied to religion, the Catholic church developed its own parochial schools. Catholics were not the only religious group to do this, but they were the largest and the strongest.[16]

The struggle over the issue of aid to education, therefore, must be seen as elements of a more fundamental debate about the understanding of religion and society. For Baptists, governmental subsidies to religiously affiliated institutions, especially those with required sectarian religious training, were equivalent to forming an established church. By doing this the state involved itself in the determination of valid forms of religious life, and by supporting those forms financially put its stamp on them. As one Baptist editor saw it, "Mixing tax dollars with church dollars is just another way of subsidizing a church which will become a puppet of the state. Church-state separation may be expensive but it is worth it."[17]

While many might argue that Baptist opposition to aid to private elementary and secondary schools was easy since they operated few such schools, the same was not true of colleges and hospitals. The first major issues regarding the latter resulted from the passage of the Hill-Burton Act in 1949. The original version of the act provided for grants of federal monies to private hospitals for use in expansion, research, and construction. This was strongly opposed by most Baptists, who felt that giving money to denominational institutions was a direct violation of the establishment clause of the First Amendment.[18] This position was so strong that the Baptist General Convention of Texas rejected the gift of a $3.5 million hospital that had been built with Hill-Burton funds.[19] As a result of lobbying by the denomination the act was later amended to include loans as well as grants. Since the loans were offered at the market rate Baptists were more willing to accept them, and many denominational hospitals eagerly did so.[20] Many hospitals, however, were unwilling to let such money go untouched. Attempts by the trustees of some of the hospitals to garner federal grants led to the separation of many of them from denominational affiliation, or at least from denominational ownership. In fact the convention itself relinquished its control over the two hospitals it owned in order that they could accept federal matching grants.

That Baptists were willing to put their beliefs on the line even at the cost of losing large sums of money is illustrated even more fully by their position regarding federal aid to higher education. The first major bill involving the allocation of federal monies to colleges and universities was the National Defense Education Act of 1958. This bill was a response to the launching of *Sputnik* by the Soviets in 1957. The major provisions of the bill affected those areas that would have had an impact on national defense—science, technology, foreign languages, and mathematics. The funding included grants to schools and individuals, as well as loans to students through the National Defense Student Loan program, later modified to the National Direct Student Loan. While the involvement of the federal government through this program was relatively limited, it raised a concern among Southern Baptists as to what—if any—degree of involvement in the program was acceptable. Baptist educators meeting in 1959 quickly voiced their opinion: loans to individual students were the only portion of the bill acceptable to them and to their institutions. Due to their principles, they willingly rejected money that would have made their jobs easier. These principles were to become sorely taxed as the involvement of the federal government and higher education increased during the 1960s.

During the Kennedy and Johnson administrations the involvement of the government with education in all its forms increased. Kennedy submitted an education bill to Congress calling for aid to public elementary and secondary schools, as well as private and public institutions of higher education. While Kennedy rejected all aid to parochial schools as unconstitutional, his position regarding colleges and universities was different. Here he was in agreement with the position of the American Council on Education. This position held that since attendance at colleges was not compulsory and since colleges functioned more in the nature of community service rather than denominational service, aid to those schools did not constitute a violation of the First Amendment.[21] Baptists, however, disagreed. On the day before it was considered by the House of Representatives the Executive Committee of the SBC passed a resolution opposing the bill. At the meeting of the convention in 1963 a resolution against direct aid to private institutions of higher education was passed as well.

> Whereas, Baptists are committed to the principle of supporting taxation for public purposes only, leaving church institutions to the voluntary support of persons desiring to participate in the support of and maintenance of those institutions; and
> Whereas we see in these principles the meaning of the "no establishment" clause of the first Amendment to the Federal Constitution as well as that of the

"Free exercise" clause of that same amendment; it is recommended, now, therefore:

1. The Southern Baptist Convention strongly opposes all legislation, federal and state, which would provide public grants to church colleges and universities for the construction of academic facilities.[22]

The Higher Education Facilities Act of 1963 passed, and Baptist colleges were confronted with the issue of how best to deal with its provisions. A complete debate over the implications of the act took place in North Carolina. Baptists there reconsidered the purpose and reasoning behind their colleges. Was education as provided by them a part of their denominational mission, or was it a public service? Some suggested that Baptists get out of the business of higher education. Baptists should remove the schools from denominational control and allow them to accept federal money.[23] The debate, therefore, centered on the issue of whether the purpose of the denominational colleges was to impart Baptist principles alongside higher education, or solely to provide the public service of education. "At this point as Baptists we will have to re-examine our purposes and decide whether under God we are called to perform a public service like education or to propagate our faith."[24]

In response to this new situation the General Board of the North Carolina Baptist Convention recommended opening the boards of trustees of the state's Baptist colleges to non-Baptists and allowing the schools to accept money for the construction of academic buildings. There was not a necessary connection between the two proposals, except that they were part of a program designed to overcome the financial problems of the schools. They became linked in the mind of the public, however, and this linkage was partially responsible for the defeat of both. First, however, it is necessary to examine the reasoning behind the proposals and the willingness of the state's denominational leadership to accept government money.

One legitimate reason for a religious institution to accept government money was that of "fee for services rendered." Under this view it was not unreasonable for an institution to accept money for a service provided, regardless of whether the payer was a private citizen or the government. A denominational hospital, therefore, would not (necessarily) be in violation of the principles of church-state separation if it accepted federal money to reimburse its costs for the care of welfare patients. Some even stretched this rationale to include the cost of research and buildings if this money was accepted in lieu of a system of reimbursement. Extrapolating from this view, some argued that private colleges also provided a service to the state and nation through their educational work, work that was subsidized by the denomination instead of by the state or federal government. Given this fact, the acceptance of federal monies was simply another case of the receipt of a fee for services rendered. It involved no excessive entanglement with government, nor did it directly further any sectarian policies. Colleges by participating in the federal program were "helping the country in what Congress has called a national emergency."[25] Because the purpose of the Higher Education Facilities Act was to meet the educational emergency of the time, participation in it was simply providing a needed public service for which the receipt of reimbursement was perfectly acceptable.

Many refused to accept the General Board in its reasoning. In fact the proposals were rejected by the annual meeting of the state convention.[26] There were many reasons for this rejection. Some resulted from long-standing conflicts within the state convention. There had been a protracted fight over the acceptance of government funds for the Baptist hospital in 1950, which resulted in the refusal of those funds—again over the recommendation of the General Board. Some of the resistance was undoubtedly related to a desire to slap down the leadership, a not uncommon occurrence. But most resistance seems to be related to principles and a deeply held rejection of government money to support denominational work.

Most who voiced opposition to the proposals and the eventual resolution opposed both proposals. Some favored the opening of the boards of trustees and rejected the federal funds. None seems to have held the opposite view, of accepting the latter and rejecting the former. Many connected their opposition to government money to their desire to retain denominational control. They felt that if the purpose of Baptist colleges was the furtherance of Baptist principles then they should be under denominational control, and if they were under denominational control they should not accept government money. They explicitly rejected the services rendered argument.

> Our schools do render valuable services. So do our churches. But are our services for sale? Are our churches in the business for the merchandising of services? The greatest service our churches or colleges can render to anyone is to win that one to Christ and train them in Christian maturity. Are we going to ask the state to pay us for rendering distinctly Christian services?[27]

Many felt that the energy should not be expended on discussing whether Baptists should take the money, but on working "for corrective legislation to stop federal grants for sectarian purposes." Baptist principles and historic

Baptist positions did not suffer in the debate either. One can often hear echoes of Leland. "Is it not a violation of conscience to ask Jews, Catholics and other sectarian groups to pay taxes that are used to support Baptist schools?"[28] Also there was the constant issue of government money bringing governmental control, despite the law's declaration that no one affiliated with the federal government could under the authority of the act "exercise any direction, supervision, or control over, or impose any requirements or conditions with respect to" the educational institution. This disclaimer was readily dispensed with. The very nature of the law was such that it exercised control over the recipients of the funds. Funds could not be used to construct buildings whose primary purpose was sectarian instruction and religious worship. As one commentator sarcastically asked, "Does 'primarily' mean you can worship a little but not much?" Acceptance of such limitations would be an egregious error. "It compartmentalizes religion. It makes distinctions in worship in the chapel and worship in the science halls."[29]

While the North Carolina State Convention voted to reject these funds only after a long struggle, other states took a much more concerted opposition to the new law (Mississippi, Texas, and Alabama). Yet it was difficult for administrators and trustees to reject such large sums of money when faced with the day-to-day obligations of making ends meet. Some schools put in requests for federal matching funds over the objections of their state conventions. An example of this was Mercer University in Georgia. The result was a long debate over whether such an action was acceptable to the Georgia State Convention. It was not. Eventually an amicable resolution was achieved: Mercer was removed from denominational control and allowed to seek its own solution to the problems of the period. Remember that the fights were over federal matching grants intended only for the construction of academic and dormitory buildings, an apparently innocuous involvement of the state with religion. Yet even here Baptists could ascertain the problems involved. If the purpose of denominational colleges was the inculcation of Baptist principles, the use of other people's tax money to assist in that enterprise would violate the principle of soul freedom. Other people's money would be used to support financially the propagation of beliefs they did not share. This was a violation not only of historic Baptist principles, but also of more recent convention positions on religious liberty. As the Southern Baptist Convention stated in the Kansas City Confession of 1963:

The church should not resort to civil power to carry on its work. The gospel of Christ contemplates spiritual means alone for the pursuit of its ends. . . . The state has no right to impose taxes for the support of any form of religion. A free church in a free state is the Christian ideal.[30]

The Higher Education Facilities Act was not, however, the only church-state issue to arise in 1963 and 1964. It was not even the major issue of those years. Most troublesome was the ruling by the Supreme Court in 1962 on what has come to be known as the Regents' Prayer Case.[31] This centered on a prayer composed by the New York State Board of Regents as part of a program of moral development for the state's public school system. The use of the prayer was left to the discretion of the local school boards. Participation was voluntary and students could be excused if they so desired. A suit was filed by the parents of ten pupils, charging that the prayer constituted a violation of the establishment clause of the First Amendment as applied to the states by the Fourteenth Amendment.

The Supreme Court's decision on behalf of the plaintiffs, followed by their ruling on required Bible reading in public schools, created an uproar over the relationship between the state and religion.[32] Many, especially in the Catholic hierarchy, felt the court was turning the country into a secular state. And with one eye on federal money to denominational schools they felt that an increasingly strict interpretation of the First Amendment would jeopardize what few opportunities they had to have private schools included in a federal aid to education bill. The ruling also was opposed by most Republicans and many Southern Democrats who were still angry over the court's rulings on civil rights. This case provided them with the opportunity to engage in court bashing without the appearance of political motivation. Southern Baptist response to the decision, however, was exceedingly favorable.

We should thank the Supreme Court for this decision simply because such a required prayer is using the government to establish religion in our public schools. This is in direct conflict with the First Amendment which guarantees that there shall be no laws passed regarding the establishment of religion. . . . For the sake of the Separation of Church and State, we should all be very happy that this legal requirement for a religious observance in public schools was not upheld.[33]

The response of the Baptist Joint Committee on Public Affairs, which had filed an *amicus curiae* brief on behalf of the plaintiffs in the Regents case, was even more positive.

We concur with the decision of the Supreme Court in *Engel v. Vitale* that prayer composed by Government officials as part of a governmental program to further religious beliefs is and should be unconstitutional. We think along with the court, that the constitutional prohibition against laws respecting an establishment of religion, must at least mean that in this country it is no part of the business of government to compose official prayers for any group of the American people to recite as part of a religious program carried on by government.[34]

Perhaps the strongest Baptist statement in favor, if not the strongest of any nature, was that of the president of the Southern Baptist Convention, Herschel Hobbs. Hobbs called the decision one "of the most powerful blows in our lifetime, maybe since the Constitution was adopted, for the freedom of religion in our Nation." Because the justices had taken such a strong stand on behalf of religious liberty he felt that all who believed in the separation of church and state "should be eternally grateful to them."[35]

In opposition to the decisions, Francis Cardinal Spellman declared that:

If that simple prayer can be interpreted as violating the separation of church and state, then I too can only pray "God save the United States," for America has truly travelled far from the ideals of her founding fathers when the prayerful mention of God's holy name in a public school breaks the law of this blessed land.[36]

Representative George Andrews (D. Alabama) was neither as circumspect nor as spiritual: "They have put the Negroes in the schools and now they have driven God out."[37]

The court's decision was an opportunity for several interest groups to attempt to further their goals. For the Catholic church it presented a chance to defend its position on federal aid to parochial schools as well as to present its position on the relationship between church and state. *America*, a leading Catholic journal, argued that the decision gave rise to a clear and logical corollary: "equal aid to all schools." This was demanded by the court's attempts to organize the public school system so that God was to be ignored. Those parents who desired a religious orientation in their children's education "should not be victimized." School aid should be given to the benefit of "all parents of all children in all schools." This was demanded by "[r]eligious freedom and civic equality."[38]

For others it provided an opportunity to engage in attacks upon the court and to gain political mileage out of what was seen as an exceedingly unpopular decision. The quote by Representative Andrews is fairly illustrative of the reasons many people took this opportunity to attack the court. Anger at the decisions on integration and civil rights in general could find a relatively safe outlet in attacks upon the court for engaging in a "deliberate and carefully planned conspiracy to substitute materialism for spiritual values."[39]

Those opposing the court's decision, regardless of the reasons, found common ground in the various constitutional amendments offered to circumvent that decision. The amendment that received the greatest hearing was the Becker Amendment, named for its author, Representative Frank Becker (R. New York).

Given the fusion of other issues with the court's decisions in *Engel* and *Schempp* one might expect to find a wide variety of opinions from Southern Baptists. This would be a reasonable expectation especially in light of the exceedingly mixed responses of the denomination's membership on racial issues and the willingness of many politicians to fuse the court's decisions on civil rights with its decisions on prayer and Bible reading in the public schools. This was not the case, however. Although Senator Strom Thurmond offered the petition of one South Carolina Baptist association in favor of the prayer amendment as illustrative of the difference between the position of the Baptist Joint Committee and the majority of Baptists, such a position was rare. All the state conventions opposed the various amendments, although in Georgia the vote was close.[40] Just as they continued to oppose the acceptance of federal grants to operate their schools, Baptists continued to oppose the various prayer amendments introduced in Congress, and maintained their support of the court on this issue.

> The Supreme Court did not order God out of the School room. It said only that the law cannot demand an invitation for him to enter. . . . Any rush into amending any part of the Bill of Rights may well create more problems than we solve. To allow prescribed prayer is no more different than allowing prescribed religion.[41]

The editor of the *Baptist Standard* was even more forceful:

> It does appear that Baptists, of all people, should realize how precious and necessary this religious freedom is and how essential it is that we oppose any slight change in the Amendment that guarantees it to us. Any change whatever in the wording of the First Amendment could easily lead to a re-examination of all court decisions made on the basis of it in the past. It is conceivable that the

addition of just a few words could eventuate in the destruction of constitutional separation of church and state.[42]

Some Baptists, however, voiced fear of and opposition to the court's decision. Among these was Billy Graham, who was "shocked and disappointed" by the decision and called it "another step toward secularism in the United States."[43] Even a minister of the status of Graham could not avoid criticism from the Baptist press for his position on this issue. The editor of the *Biblical Recorder* was not subtle when he stated, "To put it bluntly, Billy Graham almost talks out of both sides of his mouth on the prayer amendment." At the meeting of the convention in 1963 Graham was quoted as "re-iterating his stand in favor of the prayer amendment." The next day, however, a note appeared in the boxes of all the reporters covering the convention stating that "Dr. Graham was in favor of the First Amendment and had taken no stand on the Becker (prayer) Amendment."[44] That the editor was more than willing to take a few shots at Graham, a favorite of Baptists and a North Carolina native son, is suggestive of the intensity with which many Baptists held their opposition to the prayer amendment.

That a denomination that is exceedingly evangelical and overwhelmingly conservative theologically could maintain its historical position on church-state separation in the face of such vituperative attacks on the court's decision and on those opposed to the amendment is in itself quite interesting. The terms used to describe the court's decision ranged from "unmitigated blasphemy" to "regrettable." Perhaps the most complete scoring of the decision was the one that called it, "a stupid decision, a doctrinaire decision, an unrealistic decision, a decision which spits in the face of our history, our tradition, and our heritage as a religious people." Finally, if it were not enough that the decision was bad, Representative L. Mendel Rivers (D. South Carolina) vituperated that the court had "now officially stated its disbelief in God Almighty."[45]

This Southern Baptist opposition to the prayer amendment was maintained despite the fact that the representatives and senators who were most vocal and vicious in their opposition were from the Southern states.[46] These must cause one seriously to consider the nature of the issue and the ability of the denomination to respond to it. Its outspokenness on religious liberty issues a sharp contrast to its exceedingly weak witness on civil rights. The differences in the responses must say something about the denomination's theological, historical, and sociological roots. Certainly one of the main reasons for the Southern Baptist Convention's weakness on civil rights was the socialization of its membership into the values of Southern society. It is not that the denomination was necessarily in cultural captivity, but its identification with the South and the fact that the overwhelming majority of its membership was from the South affected its ability and willingness to witness to this issue.

Another factor that has been singularly absent from analysis of Southern Baptists and the issue of race is the legitimate fear for the safety of pastors. This reasoning arose in analyses of other religious institutions in the South, but no one has attributed it either to the Baptists or to moderate Southerners as a whole.[47] Yet it did not go without mention in discussions of the time. Many seemed equally afraid of destroying the denomination by too strong a statement on racial issues.[48] Similar fears did not have an impact on the convention's actions in the church-state arena primarily because the hostility was not of that magnitude. The possibility of being fired or killed because of one's opposition to the Becker Amendment was slim.

Religious liberty has been a Baptist trademark from the beginning. The sources from which the convention and Southern Baptists could draw were deep. But in the area of race Baptists could feel that they were meeting their obligations as Christians without challenging the social system. Southern Baptists fundamentally lacked the theological sources necessary to meet the social demands of the age. Their relative weakness in responding to civil rights, however, was also their strength in the cause of religious liberty. Since they felt the purpose of the state and religion were different it was not within the purview of religious bodies to actively engage in political affairs. This is not to say that they could never be involved. Religious institutions do have an obligation to speak on issues that violate the prerogatives of God. Any issue that attempted to coerce conscience was available for response since "We must obey God rather than men." However, as the powers that be are ordained of God, fundamental resistance to the social order is not within the Baptist realm of thinking, unless the civil order impinges upon the religious realm.

> We acknowledge ourselves to be citizens of two commonwealths, one earthly, the United States, the other heavenly, the Kingdom of God; and we claim the right to be good citizens of both. We recognize the sovereignty of the state and we give allegiance to the state, but we cannot give to the state the control of our consciences. We must obey God rather than men.
>
> The government resorts to coercion; we use persuasion. The government has authority over the acts of its citizens; we have to do with their motives.[49]

Baptists do not have the tradition of resistance to political evils that they have to invasions of the human conscience. While they feel that it was freely within their right to recommend certain policies to the membership, and even to petition the government in favor of these policies, they always fear the possible results of a too strong involvement in political affairs. Such an involvement holds within it the threat of church-state union. It especially holds the possibility of a rampant ecclesiasticism, which Baptists view with horror. The possibility of the church writing laws was something no Baptist can view with equanimity. Such actions result in violence to individual consciences. Regardless of how they might have viewed the morality of segregation, and the convention issued several very strong pronouncements in favor of racial equality, the structures of white supremacy were political structures that could be changed only through political action. There were no theological sources upon which they could draw in order to challenge its existence other than to inform the membership of its obligations under the rulership of Christ and to recommend that they work for better understanding between the races.

> We . . . shall strive to the end that our friends and neighbors of the Negro race shall have, in all instance, equal and impartial justice before the courts; better and more equitable opportunities in industrial, business, and professional engagements; and a more equitable share in public funds and more adequate opportunities in the field of educatioᵢ.
>
> In one word, if the spirit of the Lord and Saviour Jesus Christ is allowed to control each one of us in his relations and attitudes to all people of all races, and if our bearing and behavior are marked by the fine consideration and courtesy that Christian people are supposed to manifest, the racial problem will soon disappear.[50]

These statements, while forward looking and moderately impressive, are neither as strong nor as forceful as a comparable Baptist statement on religious liberty would have been. To find such statements one need not go back to the years of Leland. They can be found quite readily in this period.

> God alone is Lord of the conscience, and he has left it free from the doctrines and commandments of men which are contrary to his Word or not contained in it. Church and state should be separate. . . . The state has no right to impose penalties for religious opinions of any kind. The state has no right to impose taxes for the support of any form of religion. A free church in a free state is the Christian ideal, and this implies the right of free and unhindered access to God on the part of all men and the right to form and propagate opinions in the sphere of religion without interference by the civil power.[51]

It is equally important that the only institution affiliated with the Southern Baptist Convention explicitly endowed with the task of lobbying is the Public Affairs Committee. The body engaged in guaranteeing the maintenance of religious liberty is the only one of the affiliated bodies directed by the convention actively to attempt to influence legislation. The Christian Life Commission, which superseded the Social Service Commission, is not so enabled. This says something about priorities. More important, though, it tells us about their understanding of the relationship between the political realm and the religious. It also tells us of their reluctance to become too involved, as a religious institution, with the affairs of state. To an extent, therefore, the sources that give Baptists their strength in the realm of religious liberty are also partially responsible for their weakness on other issues. For all intents and purposes this manifested itself as a weakness when it came to directing the restructuring of racial relationships in the years 1930 to 1980.

There were other reasons as well. Baptists, and especially Southern Baptists by some ironic quirk, have never gotten over their feelings as theological outsiders. Their view of the world is still sectlike. Their doctrine of creation is such that they do not feel compelled to withdraw from the world. Still, they view the world as somehow alien and forbidding. Evil lurks everywhere, and Satan actively seeks to thwart the will of God. While the endeavor to improve society is indeed "a fruit of the gospel" and it would be "even impossible for our Lord to really save men without implanting in them" the impulse to serve "suffering humanity," such activity is not the first or preeminent step.

> No effort for sobriety; for civic righteousness; for economic welfare; for industrial justice; for the suppression of evil in any form in the body social or body politic, must lessen our faith in and devotion to the gospel of Christ at the first point of approach to a lost world, which is the individual heart.[52]

This feeling of being outside the mainstream, which engenders to a degree their fight for religious liberty, precludes to an extent their involvement in the affairs of state. Southern Baptists have failed fundamentally to recognize the sources of their strength and its magnitude. Far from exercising any hegemony over the Southland, Southern Baptists have often perceived themselves as an embattled righteous remnant.[53] Certainly their numerical abundance gave them the ability to predominate in certain ways, but they failed to see that predominance. Even more important, they were unable to understand how they could use it in the public realm. Certainly there were many reasons for this, not the least being the decentralized nature of the institution. Even beyond the structural level they could not see that they did or even could lead by more than example. Baptists could provide a Christian example for behavior and civic responsibility, but nothing more—at least not as Baptists. A righteous remnant does not lead an army to do battle for the Lord; it defensively protects the garden from the encroachments of Satan.

The late 1970s, however, saw attempts to force a retreat from these time-honored Baptist positions on religious liberty. The sources of this movement and its partial victories are intimately related to the rising Fundamentalist movement. The political turmoil of the 1960s and 1970s, which changed the United States as a whole, had an even greater impact on the Southern states. These events also provided a rationale for the increased polarization of the country. Compromise fell into disfavor and became increasingly rare.[54] Not only did politics as the "art of the possible" suffer, so did an institution like the SBC, the structure of which was premised to a great extent on the possibility of compromise and agreement. The increased development of single-issue groups and the rise of organizations like the Moral Majority also had an impact on the denomination and worked to restructure its historical positions and views. By the late 1970s the most outspoken Southern Baptists were those whose positions on issues were not Baptist at all. They could not be considered Baptists in any form other than name. Those people who were affiliated with the rise of Fundamentalism within the denomination favored many positions in opposition to traditional Baptist doctrine, including the adoption of a so-called school prayer amendment.

The ability of these people to gain control of the denomination was the result of the social upheaval the country experienced from 1930 through 1980. The restructuring of economic, political, and social relationships brought to the fore the complexity of differences and the competing voices that previously existed yet had remained hidden or unimportant given the relative isolation of communities, especially in the South, prior to the advent of routine air travel and telecommunications. Polarization worked against moderates in the Southern Baptist Convention, who were committed to the old order of discussion and compromise. Their commitment to the denomination put them at a disadvantage against those who felt the denomination was nothing more than a tool, a net for catching converts as one put it, which should be cleansed whenever it became contaminated. The moderation shown by those committed to the denomination was increasingly overwhelmed by those who wanted either agreement or separation. In this case the conservatives with political and religious opinions in opposition to traditional Baptist views were trying to run the moderates out of town. Increasingly the Baptist doctrines of soul freedom and religious liberty became less important, as efforts toward doctrinal conformity and support for prayer amendments made them look less and less like Baptists.

The very existence of such a movement is illustrative of the fact that changes have occurred. As one sociological observer of fundamentalism in the SBC put it, "When traditional beliefs cease to be a part of the everyday tapestry of culture, they become the agenda for a movement."[55] The biggest element of this movement is that it challenges the Baptist character of the denomination. Its emphasis on doctrinal conformity and its acceptance of the involvement of the government in religious affairs put it outside the realm of traditional Baptist doctrine and practice. The long-term success of Southern Baptist Fundamentalism is questionable. It is moving against the tide of changes, in fact against those very changes to which it owes its existence.

The eventual failure of the Fundamentalists, however, will result not from a growth of pluralism in the convention as many observers claim, but from a return to the pluralism that existed previously. The Southern Baptist Convention always has been a complex and plural institution based on compromise and consensus. The breakdown of compromise and the development of single-issue politics destroyed the bases for the convention's operation. The way was opened for groups willing to manipulate a theological conservatism into political power by playing on people's fears. This is the situation of the present. It cannot hold, however, and the final answer depends on whether Southern Baptists can return to their traditional position of accommodation, putting aside all differences for the goal of spreading the gospel.

Notes

INTRODUCTION

1. Max Horkheimer and Theodor Adorno, *Dialectic of Enlightenment* (New York: Seabury Press, 1972), p. 112.
2. Blanche McCrary Boyd, *The Redneck Way of Knowledge* (New York: Alfred A. Knopf, 1982), p. 7.
3. Quoted in George B. Tindall, *The Ethnic Southerners* (Baton Rouge: Louisiana State University Press, 1976), p. 12.
4. Maury Maverick, *A Maverick American* (New York: Covici-Friede Publishers, 1937), p. 15.
5. Willie Morris, *Terrains of the Heart and Other Essays on Home* (Oxford, Miss.: Yoknapatawpha Press, 1981), p. 33.
6. See Walter B. Shurden, *Not a Silent People: Controversies That Have Shaped Southern Baptists* (Nashville: Broadman Press, 1972).
7. For a detailed examination of this struggle see Joe Edward Barnhart, *The Southern Baptist Holy War* (Austin: Texas Monthly Press, 1986).

CHAPTER ONE

1. That Baptists are Protestants was rejected by the Landmark movement. Those belonging to this movement claimed it was possible to establish an unbroken line of churches practicing believers' baptism (immersion) back to the apostles. Only those within this lineage had a right to the name "church." That is to say that only Baptists could have churches. Other denominations might contain Christians, but were not churches. Communion was to be close, that is, allowed only to other Baptists and occasionally reserved only for members of the congregation, all interdenominationalism was eschewed, and a radical antiassociationalism held. Since early groups practicing immersion had preceded the Reformation, and the Roman Catholic Church as well, Baptists were not Protestants. Protestants were those who had broken away from the Roman church to which Baptists had never belonged.
2. Douglas Johnson, ed., *Churches and Church Membership in the United States* (Atlanta: Glenmary Research Center, 1974), pp. 32-38.

3. See Samuel S. Hill, Jr., *Southern Churches in Crisis* (New York: Holt, Rinehart and Winston, 1967).
4. Ibid., p. 33.
5. See Robert A. Baker, *The Southern Baptist Convention and its People* (Nashville: Broadman Press, 1974), and William Wright Barnes, *The Southern Baptist Convention, 1845-1953* (Nashville: Broadman Press, 1954).
6. See E. Y. Mullins, *Baptist Beliefs* (Philadelphia: The Judson Press, 1925), pp. 62-67 for a more complete statement of this.
7. *Annual of the Southern Baptist Convention, 1980*, p. 26. Cited hereafter as *SBC Annual*.
8. J. D. Grey. "Debate, Discussion for Decision, not Division," *Baptist History and Heritage* 12 (October 1977): 231.
9. J. Wayne Flynt, "One in the Spirit, Many in the Flesh: Southern Evangelicals," in *Varieties of Southern Evangelicalism*, ed. David Edwin Harrell (Macon: Mercer University Press, 1981), p. 28.
10. Ibid., p. 29.
11. *Encyclopedia of Religion in the South* (Macon: Mercer University Press, 1984), s.v. "Southern Baptist Convention," by Walter B. Shurden, p. 722.
12. Mullins, *Baptist Beliefs*, p. 64.
13. See William R. Estep, "Thomas Helwys: Bold Architect of Baptist Policy on Church-State Relations," *Baptist History and Heritage* 20 (July 1985): 24-33.
14. *The Alabama Baptist*, 5 September 1963, p. 3.
15. See Sydney Ahlstrom, *A Religious History of the American People* (New Haven: Yale University Press, 1972), pp. 317-23.
16. Rhys, Isaac, *The Transformation of Virginia, 1740-1790* (Chapel Hill: The University of North Carolina Press, 1982), pp. 162-66, 290-93.
17. Ahlstrom, *Religious History*, pp. 324, 443; see also Wayne Flynt, "One in the Spirit," p. 27.
18. Deuteronomy 25:4; Acts 8:18-24. While the most common exegesis of the citation from Acts is not that one cannot accept money for religious work, only that one cannot purchase the gifts of God which are given freely, there remains the possibility for the former interpretation.
19. See Donald G. Mathews, *Religion in the Old South* (Chicago: University of Chicago Press, 1977), pp. 192-95, 205.
20. Brooks Hays, *Politics is My Parish* (Baton Rouge: Louisiana State University Press, 1981), p. 67.
21. Baker, *The Southern Baptist Convention*, pp. 157-58.
22. Ibid., p. 155.
23. Ibid.
24. Victor I. Masters, "Baptists and the Christianizing of America in the New Order," *Review and Expositor* 17 (July 1920): 297.
25. J. Frank Norris, quoted in James J. Thompson, Jr., *Tried as By Fire: Southern Baptists and the Religious Controversies of the 1920's* (Macon: Mercer University Press, 1982), p. 20.

26. See the *Baptist Standard* (Texas), 15 April 1970, p. 14 for a story on the rich young ruler. For the statement on foreign aid see *The Alabama Baptist*, 28 July 1960, p. 3.
27. *Sunday School Young People* 15 (April-June 1950): 10; see also July-September 1950, p. 11; and *Sunday School Adults* 50 (January-March 1950): 8-10.
28. Mullins, *Baptist Beliefs*, pp. 26-29.
29. Ibid., p. 64.
30. Ibid.
31. The issue here is whether civil authorities have the right to enforce both tables of the Decalogue. The traditional Baptist response is that the first table has to do with the individual's relationship to God and is thereby outside of the competency of the magistrates. The second table, however, has to do with the individual's relationships to others in human society. It thereby falls within the purview of the state. This involves only the ability of the state to protect its members, not the religious implications of the second table of the Decalogue, which the state might enforce regardless of whether it accepted the religious source or no.
32. Thomas Helwys, *The Mistery of Iniquity* (Oxford: The Kingsgate Press, 1935), p. xxiv.

CHAPTER TWO

1. John Shelton Reed, *The Enduring South: Subcultural Persistence in Mass Society* (Chapel Hill: University of North Carolina Press, 1974), p. 89.
2. Ulrich B. Phillips, "The Central Theme of Southern History," *American Historical Review* 35 (1928): 30-43.
3. Lewis M. Killian, *White Southerners* (New York: Random House, 1970), p. 9.
4. *Harvard Encyclopedia of Ethnic Groups* (Cambridge: Harvard University Press, 1980), s.v. "Southerners," by John Shelton Reed, p. 944.
5. For an insightful discussion on immigration and ethnicity in the United States see Arthur Mann, *The One and the Many* (Chicago: University of Chicago Press, 1979).
6. The Democratic Party in the South was the "lily-white" party until the overturn of the all-white primary in 1944 (*Smith v. Allwright*, 321 U.S. 649). The phrase was used to remind everyone, as though they needed it, of the Democratic Party's difference from the Republican Party, to which those few black Southerners involved in politics belonged. The nickname of the latter was the "black and tan" party.
7. Nullification was the doctrine that the separate states could nullify any act of the federal government not specifically delegated to it and removed from the states. Interposition closely followed this line of reasoning. Here it was claimed that the state government was within its rights to interpose its authority between the Federal Government and the citizens of the state. Finally, in the theory of the

concurrent majority it was claimed, following a thought of John C. Calhoun, that different groups or regions may come together and express political views or opinions that taken together have precedence over a simple numerical majority. Under this view, groups injuriously affected by an law must accede to it for it to be enforced, like requiring robbers to agree to the outlawing of theft. "Some say that they favor interposition yet are opposed to nullification. This is like saying that we favor the aiming and firing of our guns but we are against hitting the target."

8. See C. Vann Woodward, *Origins of the New South, 1877-1913* (Baton Rouge: Louisiana State University Press, 1951), pp. 175ff.; and James L. Sellers, "The Economic Incidence of the Civil War in the South," *Mississippi Valley Historical Review* 14 (1927-28): 183-89.

9. While the number and length of imprisonments were relatively short—Jefferson Davis, the longest imprisoned, served eighteen months—the number disfranchised and killed was enormous. Some of the Confederate high command, like Robert E. Lee, never regained the rights of citizenship while alive. Others, like Judah P. Benjamin, the Confederacy's secretary of state, and John C. Breckinridge, the secretary of war, emigrated to Europe. Six thousand confederates emigrated to Brazil, two thousand left for Mexico, and hundreds went to Venezuela and British Honduras. For more information see Thomas L. Connelly and Barbara L. Bellows, *God and General Longstreet: The Lost Cause and the Southern Mind* (Baton Rouge: Louisiana State University Press, 1982), pp. 8-11.

10. This, of course, speaks only to the consequences of the war and how Southerners understood Reconstruction. It is not my view of the Reconstruction era. For a position very close to mine see Eric Foner, *Reconstruction: America's Unfinished Revolution, 1863-1877* (New York: Harper & Row, 1988).

11. C. Vann Woodward, *The Burden of Southern History* (Baton Rouge: Louisiana State University Press, 1960), pp. 95ff; see also Foner, *Reconstruction*.

12. Woodward, *Origins*, p. 304.

13. Quoted ibid., p. 312.

14. Quoted ibid., p. 316.

15. George B. Tindall, *The Emergence of the New South: 1913-1946* (Baton Rouge: Louisiana State University Press, 1967), pp. 359-60.

16. Ibid., p. 355. By the start of the economic depression in 1929, the South had already been in an agricultural depression for several years.

17. William Faulkner, *Intruder in the Dust* (New York: Random House, 1948), p. 153.

18. H. L. Mencken, "The Sahara of the Bozart," in *A Mencken Chrestomathy* (New York: Alfred A. Knopf, 1949); Mencken quoted in Tindall, *Emergence*, p. 210.

19. Twelve Southerners, *I'll Take My Stand: The South and the Agrarian Tradition* (Gloucester, Mass.: Peter Smith, 1976).

20. John Crowe Ransom, "Reconstructed but Unregenerate," ibid., p. 9.

21. Quoted in Woodward, *Burden*, p. 32.

22. United States Department of Commerce, Bureau of the Census, *Statistical Abstract of the United States, 1938* (Washington, D.C.: Government Printing Office, 1938), p. 7, illus. #9.
23. Charles P. Roland, *The Improbable Era: The South Since World War II* (Lexington: University Press of Kentucky, 1975), pp. 22-25.
24. Ibid., p. 71.
25. For court cases see *Baker v. Carr*, 369 U.S. 186.; *Reynolds v. Simms*, 377 U.S. 533.; *Wesberry v. Sanders*, 376 U.S. 1.
26. Boyd, *The Redneck Way of Knowledge*, p. 5.
27. Roy Blount, Jr., "C'mon, They're Not All Dumber than Two-Dollar Dogs," *TV Guide*, 2 February 1980, p. 8-10.
28. The presence at Selma of a large number of ministers and celebrities from outside the state is a good example of this. The ability of the media to make the events there present to hand and the ease of travel were possible only in our time. Without the coverage and the ability to be present there would have been no help.
29. See Tindall, *Emergence*, p. 541.
30. W. E. B. DuBois, quoted ibid.
31. Ibid. See also Richard L. Watson, Jr., "The Defeat of Judge Parker: A Study in Pressure Groups and Politics," *Mississippi Valley Historical Review* 50 (1963-1964): 213-34.
32. C. Vann Woodward. *The Strange Career of Jim Crow*, 3rd rev. ed. (New York: Oxford University Press, 1974), pp. 117-18.
33. Lillian Smith, *Killers of the Dream* (New York: Norton, 1949), p. 90.
34. J. Morgan Kousser, *The Shaping of Southern Politics: Suffrage Restriction and the Formation of the One Party South, 1880-1910* (New Haven: Yale University Press, 1974).
35. See V. O. Key, Jr., *Southern Politics in State and Nation* (New York: Knopf, 1949).
36. Quoted in Jack Bass and Walter DeVries, *The Transformation of Southern Politics* (New York: Basic Books, 1976), p. 58.
37. For an eloquent statement of the effect of segregation on the former see Martin Luther King, Jr., "Letter from a Birmingham Jail," in Martin Luther King, Jr., *Why We Can't Wait* (New York: Harper & Row, 1963).
38. Robert Coles, *Children of Crisis* (Boston: Little, Brown and Company, 1967), pp. 272-73.
39. Ibid., pp. 273-74.
40. John Howard Griffin, *Black Like Me* (New York: Signet, 1976), pp. 92-94.

CHAPTER THREE

1. Louis D. Rubin, Jr., "The Boll Weevil, the Iron Horse, and the End of the Line: Thoughts on the South," in *The American South: Portrait of a Culture*, ed. Louis D. Rubin, Jr. (Baton Rouge: Louisiana State University Press, 1980), p. 368.
2. John Shelton Reed, "Instant Grits and Plastic-Wrapped Crackers: Southern Culture and Regional Development," ibid., p. 29.
3. Quoted in George B. Tindall, *The Ethnic Southerners* (Baton Rouge: Louisiana State University Press, 1976), p. 43.
4. Ibid., p. 15.
5. Quoted in Paul Binding, *Separate Country: A Literary Journey Through the American South* (New York: Paddington Press, Ltd., 1979), p. 186.
6. Reed, *The Enduring South*, p. 33.
7. Tindall, *The Ethnic Southerners*, p. 11.
8. Reed, "Instant Grits," p. 29.
9. Fred Hobson, *Tell About the South: The Southern Rage to Explain* (Baton Rouge: Louisiana State University Press, 1983), pp. 328-29.
10. C. Vann Woodward, *Thinking Back: The Perils of Writing History* (Baton Rouge: Louisiana State University Press, 1986), p. 109.
11. Mary M. Colum, quoted in F. Garvin Davenport, Jr., *The Myth of Southern History: Historical Consciousness in Twentieth-Century Southern Literature* (Nashville: Vanderbilt University Press, 1970), p. 116.
12. See William C. Havard, Jr., "Southern Politics: Old and New Style," in Rubin, *American South*, pp. 57-58. These characteristics are borne out as much in social scientific research as they are in literature. Southerners show a greater interest in state and local politics than in national and international affairs, are more likely to name a family member or neighbor as the biggest influence on their lives. They are also more likely to look to their churches for guidance than are other Americans. See Reed, *Enduring South*, pp. 33-34, 39, 85, and passim.
13. Quoted in Tindall, *Ethnic Southerners*, p. 18.
14. Louis D. Rubin, Jr., *William Elliott Shoots a Bear: Essays on the Southern Literary Imagination* (Baton Rouge: Louisiana State University Press, 1975), p. 256.
15. Flannery, O'Connor, *Everything that Rises Must Converge* (New York: Farrar, Straus and Giroux, 1965); Robert Penn Warren, *Night Rider* (New York: Vintage Books, 1979); William Styron, *Sophie's Choice* (New York: Bantam Books, 1980).

   The inclusion of *Sophie's Choice* in this list is perfectly legitimate and does not detract from the issue of Southern literature even though the main character is Polish. As Louis Rubin has aptly noted, "the so-called 'southern quality' in modern American fiction is not at bottom a matter of subject matter or theme, so much as of attitude; it is a way of looking at the nature of human experience, and it includes the assumption that to maintain order and stability the individual must be part of a social community, yet that the ultimate authority that underlies his conduct is not social but moral. It is, in short, a religious attitude, though most often it does not involve the dogmas of revealed religion. This attitude, not the presence of the particular institutions and events that customarily embody the attitude, is what has enabled the work of the better southern novelists to seem so 'meaningful' in our time." Rubin, *William Elliott Shoots a Bear*, p. 230.

Styron alludes to this possibility in *Sophie's Choice* itself when in an extended analogy he compares Poland and the South (pp. 301-2). Also see "The South: Distance and Change. A Conversation with Robert Penn Warren, William Styron, and Louis D. Rubin, Jr." in Rubin, *American South*, pp. 304-22.

16. For another example of this see the character of Willie Stark in Robert Penn Warren, *All the King's Men* (San Diego: Harcourt Brace Jovanovich, 1974).
17. Louis D. Rubin, Jr., "The American South: The Continuity of Self-Definition," in Rubin, *American South*, p. 17.
18. Woodward, *Burden*, p. 18.
19. Quoted in Woodward, *Burden*, pp. 169-70.
20. Warren, *All the King's Men*, p. 438.
21. "From a broader point of view it is not the South but America that is unique among the peoples of the world. . . . The collective will of [America] has simply never known what it means to be confronted by complete frustration." Woodward, *Burden*, p. 168.
22. Faulkner, *Intruder in the Dust*, pp. 148-49.
23. Rubin, "Boll Weevil," p. 368.
24. Rubin, *William Elliott Shoots a Bear*, p. 148.
25. Ibid., pp. 148-49.
26. John Donald Wade, "Southern Humor," in *Culture in the South*, ed. W. T. Couch (Chapel Hill: University of North Carolina Press, 1935), p. 624.
27. Rubin, *William Elliott Shoots a Bear*, p. 151.
28. Ibid., p. 153.
29. For an example of this see the interchange between Stingo and Nathan regarding Theodore Bilbo in Styron, *Sophie's Choice*, pp. 248-56.
30. Rubin, *William Elliott Shoots a Bear*, p. 230.

CHAPTER FOUR

1. See Hill, *Southern Churches in Crisis*.
2. J. Herbert Gilmore, *They Chose to Live: The Racial Agony of an American Church* (Grand Rapids: Eerdmans, 1972), pp. 7-8.
3. *SBC Annual, 1964*, p. 229; *Biblical Recorder*, 4 April 1964, p. 7.
4. John Lee Eighmy, *Churches in Cultural Captivity: A History of the Social Attitudes of Southern Baptists* (Knoxville: University of Tennessee Press, 1972).
5. *SBC Annual, 1928*, p. 85.
6. See *The Alabama Baptist*, 24 March 1932, p. 3, and 7 July 1932, p. 3; *Baptist Standard* (Texas), 3 May 1934, p. 4; and *Biblical Recorder* (North Carolina), 5 April 1933, p. 7.

7. See for example *SBC Annual, 1937*, p. 72; *SBC Annual, 1938*, p. 117.
8. *SBC Annual, 1939*, p. 114.
9. Stan L. Hastey, "The History and Contributions of the Baptist Joint Committee on Public Affairs" *Baptist History and Heritage* 20 (July 1985): 37.
10. *SBC Annual, 1946*, p. 111; *SBC Annual, 1948*, p. 57; *SBC Annual, 1949*, p. 55.
11. See for example *The Alabama Baptist*, 16 January 1964, p. 7, and 22 January 1959, p. 4; *SBC Annual, 1959*, p. 140.
12. *The Alabama Baptist*, 26 November 1964, p. 8; *Biblical Recorder* (North Carolina), 1964; *Encyclopedia of Southern Baptists* (Nashville: Broadman Press, 1958-1982), v. 4, s.v. "Pate, Mavis Orisca."
13. *SBC Annual, 1956*, p. 331.
14. *SBC Annual, 1940*, p. 96.
15. See *The Alabama Baptist*, 26 July 1934, p. 5.
16. *SBC Annual, 1895*, p. 38.
17. Joseph Martin Dawson, *A Thousand Months to Remember* (Waco: Baylor University Press, 1964), pp. 160-61.
18. *Book of Reports, Southern Baptist Convention 1946*, pp. 11-12.
19. Alfred O. Hero, Jr., *The Southerner and World Affairs* (Baton Rouge: Louisiana University Press, 1965), pp. 3-10.
20. Ibid., p. 7.
21. *The Alabama Baptist*, 4 December 1968, pp. 1, 11.
22. *SBC Annual, 1979*, p. 51; *SBC Annual, 1978*, p. 54.
23. James L. Guth, "Preachers and Politics: Varieties of Activism Among Southern Baptist Ministers," in *Religion and Politics in the South*, ed. Tod A. Baker, Robert P. Steed, and Robert W. Moreland (New York: Praeger, 1983), pp. 165, 168.
24. Dawson, *A Thousand Months*, p. 261.
25. *The Alabama Baptist*, 28 January 1932, p. 3, and 11 August 1932, p. 3.
   While Gwaltney was disgusted with the behavior of American capitalists during the 1920s and felt that their monopolistic practices had resulted in the economic collapse of the country, he did not reject capitalism per se. This was especially true as he began to view the results of the anticapitalist revolutions in Germany, the Soviet Union, and Italy during the 1930s. He began to wonder whether religious and individual freedom might be possible only under some form of modified capitalism, and rarely gave an unqualified endorsement to socialism. He felt, however, that capitalism was historically dead and that a movement toward a form of democratic socialism, as in England, was inevitable for the United States. This movement he hoped could be achieved with a maintenance of as many individual liberties as possible. See L. L. Gwaltney, *The World's Greatest Decade: The Times and the Baptists* (Birmingham: Birmingham Publishing Company, 1949), p. 86.
26. *SBC Annual, 1935*, pp. 34-35.
27. *SBC Annual, 1978*, p. 58.
28. Dawson, *A Thousand Months*, p. 260.
29. Tindall, *Emergence*, p. 607.

30. Marion Montgomery, "The Enduring Faith," in *Why the South Will Survive*, ed. Fifteen Southerners (Athens: University of Georgia Press, 1981), p. 188.

31. *Sunday School Young People* 15 (April-June 1950): 10, 11-13; see also (July-September 1950): 11.

32. *Sunday School Adults* 46 (January-March 1956): 29.

33. *Sunday School Young People* 26 (January-March 1961): p. 43.

34. The former is especially true in terms of the responses of white Southerners to questions involving the activity of the federal government. To a question such as whether there should be more "federal effort to solve social problems," many white Southerners see black, as it were. Federal involvement has been a code phrase relating to federal intervention on civil rights for so long that it has begun to take on a negative life of its own to many without reference or thought to racial overtones. Its positive implications as a result of the New Deal have been largely forgotten. See Guth, "Preachers and Politics," pp. 163-65. For a discussion of the conflict between the attitudes of Southerners on race and economics see Robert Emil Botsch, *We Shall Not Overcome: Populism and Southern Blue-Collar Workers* (Chapel Hill: University of North Carolina Press, 1980), pp. 122-23, 157-62, 195-201.

35. Mrs. H. G. Dennis, letter to the editor, *The Alabama Baptist*, 9 April 1970, p. 3; see also 12 March 1970, pp. 1, 3, 5-6.

36. Bobby G. Couey, letter to the editor, ibid., 9 April 1970, p. 3.

37. Ibid.

38. *SBC Annual, 1969*, p. 69.

39. *Baptist Intermediate Quarterly I* 61 (January-March 1970); *Baptist Intermediate Quarterly II* 19 (January-March 1970).

40. W. H. Schrader, letter to the editor, *The Alabama Baptist*, 19 March 1970, p. 3.

41. Charles Williams, letter to the editor, ibid.

42. Training Union Class of Grove Hill, Alabama, letter to the editor, ibid.

43. James R. Linton, letter to the editor, ibid.

44. *SBC Annual, 1977*, p. 76.

45. See *Encyclopedia of Southern Baptists*, v. 4, s.v. "Sexuality, Human."

46. For a discussion of this conflict see Thompson, *Tried as by Fire*; and Baker, *The Southern Baptist Convention*, pp. 397-400.

47. The leaders in the attempts by Fundamentalists to take over the SBC were W. A. Criswell's associate minister at First Baptist Church, Dallas Paige Patterson, who is also president of the Criswell Center for Biblical Studies, and Judge Paul Pressler. They were responsible for organizing the concerted effort to gain control of the convention. See Leon McBeth, "Fundamentalism in the Southern Baptist Convention in Recent Years," *Review and Expositor* 79 (Winter 1982): 85-103; and Charles Allen, "Paige Patterson: Contender for Baptist Sectarianism," ibid., pp. 105-20. See also Joe Barnhart, *Southern Baptist Holy War*.

48. Guth, "Preachers and Politics, p. 162.

49. Ibid., p. 177.

50. See for example *Sunday School Young People* 15 (April-June 1950): 8-10.
51. Wilbur J. Cash, *The Mind of the South* (New York: Vintage Books, 1941), pp. 44, 46.
52. William Owen Carver, *Out of His Treasure: Unfinished Memoirs* (Nashville: Broadman Press, 1956), p. 83.
53. *Roe v. Wade*, 410 U.S. 113; 93 S. Ct. 705; 35 L. Ed. 2d 147 (1973).
54. *SBC Annual, 1971*, p. 72; *SBC Annual, 1974*, p. 76; *SBC Annual, 1976*, pp. 57-58. The resolution as printed in the 1976 convention annual is in error. It includes two paragraphs not adopted by the convention, which makes the resolution sound stronger than it is. For a record of this see the copy of the 1976 annual annotated by Porter Routh, executive secretary-treasurer of the SBC, in the possession of the Southern Baptist Historical Library and Archives. See also the statement of 10 November 1976 released to the Baptist press by Clifton J. Allen, recording secretary of the SBC.
55. See *SBC Annual, 1974*, p. 76; *SBC Annual, 1976*, pp. 57-58; *SBC Annual, 1979*, pp. 50-51.
56. *SBC Annual, 1980*, pp. 48-49.
57. *SBC Annual, 1980*, p. 49.
58. *SBC Annual, 1976*, p. 58.
59. Southern Baptists have preached and acted in opposition to alcohol for over 100 years. (Tobacco has also come under criticism and scrutiny.) In a survey of Southern Baptists administered by the Sunday School Board the drinking of alcoholic beverages was the third most important concern. It was led only by neglect of parental responsibility in raising children and reluctance of individuals to get involved over moral, social, and economic issues; it exceeded sexual immorality by 7 percentage points. Sunday School Board, *Southern Baptist Membership Survey* (Nashville: Sunday School Board, SBC, 1968), p. 40.
    James Guth has also noted that among the Southern Baptist ministers he surveyed, more saw a greater need for controlling the liquor traffic than homosexuality. Guth, "Preachers and Politics," pp. 169-71.
60. *Encyclopedia of Southern Baptists*, v. 1, s.v. "Fundamentalism."

CHAPTER FIVE

1. Cash, *Mind of the South*, p. 51; Ralph Ellison quoted in Tindall, *Ethnic Southerners*, p. 19.
2. Cash, *Mind of the South*, p. 40.
3. Some political radicals also played upon racial fears in their struggles with entrenched political elites. The best example of this was Theodore Bilbo of Mississippi. See Chester M. Morgan, *Redneck Liberal: Theodore G. Bilbo and the New Deal* (Baton Rouge: Louisiana State University Press, 1985). This was rare, however, and most used the issue of race to hide political failures and unkept promises. Two example of this are Eugene Talmadge and George C. Wallace. See

William Anderson, *The Wild Man from Sugar Creek* (Baton Rouge: Louisiana State University Press, 1975), and Marshall Frady, *Wallace* (New York: The World Publishing Company, 1968).

4. Throughout the nineteenth century Senator Henry Cabot Lodge continued to push for the passage of the so-called Force Bill, which would have returned federal overseers to the states of the former Confederacy in order to guarantee blacks the franchise. Southern politicians played up this threat as a return to the Reconstruction era when Union troops occupied the Southern states.

5. Quoted in Anthony P. Dunbar, *Against the Grain: Southern Radical and Prophets, 1929-1950* (Charlottesville: University Press of Virginia, 1981), p. 86.

6. See for example *The Alabama Baptist*, 4 May 1961, p. 3, 8 June 1961, p. 3, and 14 February 1963, p. 3.

7. For a more complete discussion of this issue see David T. Bailey, *Shadow on the Church: Southwestern Evangelical Religion and the Issue of Slavery, 1783-1860* (Ithaca: Cornell University Press, 1985).

8. Quoted in *Baptist Standard* (Texas), 9 February 1972, p. 4.

9. Ibid., 18 February 1959, p. 15.

10. *Plessy v. Ferguson*, 163 U.S. 537 (1896).

11. Quoted in *Baptist Standard* (Texas), 1 June 1960, p. 12.

12. *Sunday School Young People* 27 (January-March 1962): 16.

13. *Biblical Recorder* (North Carolina), 29 May 1954, p. 5.

14. *Baptist Standard* (Texas), 10 June 1954, p. 2.

15. *SBC Annual, 1954*, p. 56.

16. Mathews, *Religion in the Old South*, p. 152.

17. Quoted in Ralph McGill, *The South and the Southerner* (Boston: Little, Brown and Company, 1963), p. 217.

18. Arthur Barton, "Report on Inter-racial Relations," quoted in *Biblical Recorder* (North Carolina), 3 May 1933, p. 14.

19. See Thompson, *Tried as By Fire*, pp. 101-36.

20. *The Alabama Baptist*, 17 November 1932, p. 4; *Biblical Recorder* (North Carolina), 19 April 1933, p. 11, and 26 April 1933, p. 7.

21. Reed, *The Enduring South*, pp. 62-63.

22. *Baptist Standard* (Texas), 18 August 1932, p. 4. For a further statement on Southern personalism see Samuel S. Hill, Jr., "The Shape and Shapes of Popular Southern Piety," in Harrell, *Varieties of Southern Evangelicalism*, pp. 111-12.

23. *The Alabama Baptist*, 11 October 1963, p. 3.

24. Ibid., 21 March 1968, p. 13.

25. *Sunday School Young People* 27 (January-March 1962): 31.

26. Ibid., p. 50.

27. *The Alabama Baptist*, 11 October 1962, p. 3, and 30 July 1964, p. 3.

28. Ibid., 24 January 1963, p. 7.

29. Ibid., 22 November 1962, p. 9.

30. Campbell was a white Mississippian, a Baptist minister, and a special observer on racial affairs of the National Council Churches during the height of the civil rights movement.
31. Will Campbell, *Brother to a Dragonfly* (New York: Continuum, 1977), p. 220.
32. See *The Alabama Baptist*, 1 October 1970, p. 6; and Gilmore, *They Chose to Live*.
33. Mrs. Margaret Maynard, letter to the editor, *The Alabama Baptist*, 4 April 1968, p. 4.
34. Mrs. Bill Paris, letter to the editor, ibid.
35. Ibid., 8 June 1961, p. 3.
36. Ibid., 26 September 1963, p. 3.
37. Mrs. Creed Gilbreath, letter to the editor, ibid., 27 August 1964, p. 4.
38. James C. McCary, letter to the editor, ibid., 27 September 1964, p. 4.
39. Quoted in ibid., 18 July 1968, p. 13. Criswell previously had been a staunch proponent of segregation. He announced his change of heart in a sermon before Dallas's First Baptist Church in 1968. See W. A. Criswell, "The Church of the Open Door," in *Baptists See Black*, ed. Wayne Dehoney (Waco: Word Books, 1969), pp. 73-82. It was equally a politic move for him, being touted as he was for the convention's presidency, to remove any hint of scandal from his person.
40. *The Alabama Baptist*, 11 October 1962, p. 3.
41. The Men's Sunday School Class of Robinson Springs Baptist Church, letter to the editor, ibid., 1 January 1970, p. 3. This was the most disturbing letter I discovered during my research, for I knew those men. They were the leaders in the community in which I was raised, who led me as a youth. The pain caused by seeing them behave like that is like discovering a horrible secret about a parent.
42. Ibid., 30 July 1964, p. 3.
43. Ibid., 4 May 1961, p. 3.
44. Ibid., 11 October 1962, p. 3.
45. See *Baptist Standard* (Texas), 9 February 1972, p. 3.
46. Ibid., 9 February 1972, p. 4.
47. Ibid., 30 July 1964, p. 3.
48. Jean Baugh, missionary to East Pakistan (now Bangladesh), quoted in *Biblical Recorder* (North Carolina), 30 May 1964, p. 17.
49. Bill J. Leonard, "Southern Baptists and Southern Culture," *American Baptist Quarterly* 4 (June 1985): 209.

CHAPTER SIX

1. See Isaac, *Transformation of Virginia*, pp. 166-77, for a discussion of the impact of the Baptists on Virginia in the eighteenth century. For a discussion of Baptists in Massachusetts see William G. McLoughlin *New England Dissent, 1630-1833:*

The Baptists and the Separation of Church and State, 2 vols. (Cambridge: Harvard University Press, 1971).

2. John Leland, "The Rights of Conscience Inalienable, and, therefore Religious Opinions not Cognizable by Law: Or, The Highflying Churchman, Stripped of his Legal Robe, Appears a Yaho," in *The Writings of the Late Elder John Leland, including Some Events in His Life* (New York: G. W. Wood, 1845), p. 181.
3. John Leland, "The Virginia Chronicle," ibid., p. 114.
4. Leland, "Rights of Conscience," p. 184.
5. See Leland, "Virginia Chronicle," pp. 118-20. For Leland's statement regarding the nature and form of government see "Rights of Conscience," pp. 179-80.
6. Leland, "Virginia Chronicle," p. 118.
7. See "A Pronouncement on Religious Liberty," *SBC Annual, 1939*, pp. 114-16. The "American Baptist Bill of Rights" was adopted by three different Baptist conventions, the SBC, the Northern Baptist Convention, and the National Baptist Convention, USA, as part of the formation of the Baptist Joint Committee on Public Affairs—at that time known as the Joint Conference Committee. See Hastey, "History of Baptist Joint Committee," p. 36.
8. *SBC Annual, 1939*, pp. 114-16.
9. Hastey, "History of Baptist Joint Committee," p. 36.
10. Justice Black, in writing the opinion, stated that such transportation fell within the same category as police protection at school crossings, fire protection, water and sewer facilities, highways, and sidewalks. By supplying bus transportation to these children the state of New Jersey did no more than provide public welfare legislation and, therefore, did not violate the concept of the separation of church and state. *Everson v. Board of Education*, 330 U.S. 1; 67 S. Ct. 504; 91 L. Ed. 711 (1947).
11. The only partial exception to this was the limited support given to the Elementary and Secondary Education Act of 1965 by the Baptist Joint Committee on Public Affairs. Following the "child-benefit" theory the BJCPA supported the existence of certain indirect subsidies to nonpublic schools. See Hastey, "History of Baptist Joint Committee," p. 39.
12. *Biblical Recorder* (North Carolina), 21 December 1932, p. 7; *SBC Annual, 1935*, pp. 33-34.
13. *Biblical Recorder* (North Carolina), 22 February 1964, p. 14.
14. *SBC Annual, 1963*, p. 257.
15. Even at the height of the hysteria over integration the Virginia Baptist Convention condemned its state's voucher plan as a violation of church-state separation. This was a very interesting action given the fact that Virginia had rescinded its law requiring the existence of public county schools, and at least one county, Prince Edward, closed its public schools. The voucher plan would have been very useful to those (white) parents who still intended to send their children to segregated private academies yet could not afford the cost.
16. Many have argued that the reason for the existence of Catholic education was the "Protestant" character of the public schools, but this only confuses the issue. Public schools were Protestant to the Catholic hierarchy insofar as they were not

131

Catholic, witness the intent of the church to control its own educational systems even in those countries generally considered Catholic—Spain, France, and Italy. It is perhaps more fruitful to speak of the position of the hierarchy as insisting that all education for Catholics be tied to their religion, and that any educational forms not so connected were unacceptable.

17. *Baptist Standard* (Texas), 5 July 1972, p. 2.
18. For a representative debate over the issues involved see all the issues of the *Biblical Recorder* (North Carolina) for 1950.
19. See *The Alabama Baptist*, 15 January 1959. p. 4; *Baptist Standard* (Texas), 26 August 1959, pp. 4-5; 13 January 1960, p. 14; and 3 February 1960, p. 14.
20. See Anson Phelps Stokes and Leo Pfeffer, *Church and State in the United States*, rev. one-volume ed. (New York: Harper & Row, 1964), p. 204.
21. See C. Emanuel Carlson and Barry W. Garrett, *Religious Liberty* (Nashville: Convention Press, 1964), p. 137.
22. Ibid., p. 138. See also *SBC Annual, 1963*, pp. 6, 253-54.
23. See *Biblical Recorder* (North Carolina), 1 February 1964, p. 16.
24. Ibid., 4 January 1964, p. 16.
25. Ibid., 31 October 1964, p. 10.
26. Ibid., 21 November 1964, p. 6.
27. Ibid., 10 October 1964, p. 19.
28. Ibid., 7 November 1964, p. 9.
29. Ibid., 10 October 1964, p. 19; see also 12 September 1964, p. 10.
30. *SBC Annual, 1963*, pp. 269-81. See also Memphis Confession of 1925, in *SBC Annual, 1925*, pp. 71-76.
31. *Steven I. Engel et al. v. William J. Vitale, Jr. et al.*, 370 U.S. 421; 82 S. Ct. 1261; 8 L. ed. 2d. 601 (1962).
32. The ruling against the devotional reading of the Bible in public schools came about in *School District of Abington Township v. Schempp*, 374 U.S. 203; 83 S. Ct. 1560; 10 L. Ed. 2d. 844 (1963).
33. *The Alabama Baptist*, 5 July 1962, p. 3.
34. Carlson, *Religious Liberty*, p. 107.
35. Quoted ibid., p. 108.
36. *The New York Times*, 28 June 1962, p. 17.
37. Ibid., 26 June 1962, p. 1.
38. *America*, 29 June 1963, p. 898.
39. Representative John Bell Williams (D. Mississippi), quoted in *The New York Times*, 27 June 1962, p. 1.
40. *Biblical Recorder* (North Carolina), 9 May 1964, p. 5.
41. Quoted ibid., 25 April 1964, p. 6.
42. Ibid.
43. *The New York Times*, 26 June 1962, p. 17.
44. *Biblical Recorder* (North Carolina), 30 May 1964, p. 2.

45. *The New York Times*, 18 June 1963, p. 7; Response of National Association of Evangelicals, ibid., 26 June 1962, p. 17; editorial in *The Pilot* (Diocese of Boston), quoted ibid., 27 June 1962, p. 20; Mendel Rivers quoted ibid.
46. For a discussion of the opposition see William M. Beaney and Edward N. Beiser, "Prayer and Politics: The Impact of Engel and Schempp on the Political Process," *Journal of Public Law* 13 (1964): 486-87.
47. For a discussion of how this was applied to other religious groups see Marvin Braiterman, "Mississippi Maranos," in *Jews in the South*, ed. Leonard Dinnerstein and Mary Dale Palsson (Baton Rouge: Louisiana State University Press, 1973), pp. 351-59.
48. See *Biblical Recorder* (North Carolina), 7 November 1964, p. 14; *The Alabama Baptist*, 8 January 1970, p. 6. See also Campbell, *Brother to a Dragonfly*, pp. 125-36, 156-59; and Dehoney, *Baptists See Black*, pp. 9-22, 83-94.
49. *SBC Annual, 1939*, p. 116.
50. *SBC Annual, 1941*, p. 95; *SBC Annual, 1940*, p. 127.
51. "Kansas City Confession of 1963," Section XVII, "Religious Liberty," in *SBC Annual, 1963*, pp. 269-81.
52. *SBC Annual, 1936*, p. 25.
53. Frederick Bode, in his discussion regarding the debates over state funding of higher education in North Carolina, *Protestantism and the New South: North Carolina Baptists and Methodists in Political Crisis, 1894-1903* (Charlottesville: University Press of Virginia, 1975), suggests that Baptists and Methodists in the South exercise hegemony over the region. While certain of his claims are well founded it is important to separate what is fundamentally a moral hegemony from a political hegemony. There is also a distinct difference between the actual and the perceived. Baptists have no sources upon which to draw in order to exercise that hegemony except in terms of the salvation of souls. Even the most outspoken claims of the potential of the Baptists in the South relate to world salvation, not political domination.
54. For a discussion of the collapse of reason and discussion see Wayne C. Booth, *Now Don't Try to Reason with Me: Essays and Ironies for a Credulous Age* (Chicago: University of Chicago Press, 1970).
55. Nancy T. Ammerman, quoted in *Chicago Tribune*, 13 June 1986, section 2, p. 9.

Bibliography

BAPTIST SOURCES

The Alabama Baptist
Ambassador Life
Annual of the Southern Baptist Convention
Arkansas Baptist
Baptist Intermediate Quarterly
Baptist Married Young People
The Baptist Record (Mississippi)
Baptist Standard (Texas)
Baptist Student
Baptist Training Union Magazine
Baptist Young Adults
Baptist Young People
Becoming Magazine
Biblical Recorder (North Carolina)
Book of Reports: Southern Baptist Convention
The Christian Index (Georgia)
Intermediate Pupil
Sunday School Young Adults
Sunday School Young People
Texas Baptist Oral History Consortium Memoirs

SECONDARY MATERIAL

Allen, Charles. "Paige Patterson: Contender for Baptist Sectarianism." *Review and Expositor* 79 (Winter 1982): 105-20.

Anderson, William. *The Wild Man from Sugar Creek*. Baton Rouge: Louisiana State University Press, 1975.

Badger, Anthony J. *Prosperity Road: The New Deal, Tobacco, and North Carolina*. Chapel Hill: University of North Carolina Press, 1980.

Bailey, David T. *Shadow on the Church: Southwestern Evangelical Religion and the Issue of Slavery, 1783-1860*. Ithaca: Cornell University Press, 1985.

Bailey, Kenneth K. *Southern White Protestantism in the Twentieth Century*. New York: Harper and Row, 1964.

Baker, Robert A. *The Southern Baptist Convention and its People*. Nashville: Broadman Press, 1974.

————. *A Baptist Source Book: With Particular Reference to Southern Baptists*. Nashville: Broadman Press, 1966.

Baker, Tod A., Robert P. Steed, and Robert W. Moreland, eds. *Religion and Politics in the South*. New York: Praeger, 1983.

Barnes, William Wright. *The Southern Baptist Convention, 1845-1953*. Nashville: Broadman Press, 1954.

Barnhart, Joe Edward. *The Southern Baptist Holy War*. Austin: Texas Monthly Press, 1986.

Bass, Jack, and Walter DeVries. *The Transformation of Southern Politics: Social Change and Political Consequence since 1945*. New York: Basic Books, 1976.

Beaney, William M., and Edward N. Beiser. "Prayer and Politics: The Impact of Engel and Schempp on the Political Process." *Journal of Public Law* 13 (1964): 486-87.

Belfrage, Cedric. *A Faith to Free the People*. New York: Dryden Press, 1944.

Billington, Monroe L., ed. *The South: A Central Theme?* New York: Holt, Rinehart and Winston, 1969.

Binding, Paul. *Separate Country: A Literary Journey Through the American South*. New York: Paddington Press, Ltd., 1979.

Blount, Roy, Jr. "C'mon, They're Not All Dumber than Two-Dollar Dogs," *TV Guide*, 2 February 1980, pp. 8-10.

Bode, Frederick A. *Protestantism and the New South: North Carolina Baptists and Methodists in Political Crisis, 1894-1903*. Charlottesville: University Press of Virginia, 1975.

Booth, Wayne C. *Now Don't Try to Reason with Me: Essays and Ironies for a Credulous Age*. Chicago: University of Chicago Press, 1970.

Botsch, Robert Emil. *We Shall Not Overcome: Populism and Southern Blue-Collar Workers*. Chapel Hill: University of North Carolina Press, 1980.

Boyd, Blanche McCrary. *The Redneck Way of Knowledge*. New York: Alfred A. Knopf, 1982.

Brown H. C., Jr. *Southern Baptist Preaching*. Nashville: Broadman Press, 1959.

_____. *More Southern Baptist Preaching*. Nashville: Broadman Press, 1964.

Bryan, G. McLeod. *Dissenter in the Baptist Southland: Fifty Years in the Career of William Wallace Finlator*. Macon: Mercer University Press, 1985.

Campbell, Will D. *Brother to a Dragonfly*. New York: Continuum, 1977.

Campbell, Will D. and James Y. Holloway, eds. *The Failure and the Hope: Essays of Southern Churchmen*. Grand Rapids: Eerdmans, 1972.

Carlson, C. Emanuel, and W. Barry Garrett. *Religious Liberty: Case Studies in Current Church State Issues*. Nashville: Convention Press, 1964.

Carver, William Owen. *Out of His Treasure: Unfinished Memoirs*. Nashville: Broadman Press, 1956.

Cash, Wilbur J. *The Mind of the South*. New York: Vintage Books, 1941.

Cason, Clarence. *90 in the Shade*. Chapel Hill: University of North Carolina Press, 1935.

Chadbourn, James H. *Lynching and the Law*. Chapel Hill: University of North Carolina Press, 1933.

Cobb, James C. *Industrialization and Southern Society, 1877-1984*. Lexington: University Press of Kentucky, 1984.

Cobb, James C., and Michael V. Namorato, eds. *The New Deal and the South*. Jackson: University Press of Mississippi, 1984.

Coles, Robert. *Children of Crisis*. Boston: Little, Brown and Company, 1967.

Colvert, James B. "Views of Southern Character in some Northern Novels." *Mississippi Quarterly* 18 (Spring 1965): 59-68.

Connelly, Thomas L., and Barbara L. Bellows. *God and General Longstreet: The Lost Cause and the Southern Mind*. Baton Rouge: Louisiana State University Press, 1982.

Couch, W. T., ed. *Culture in the South*. Chapel Hill: University of North Carolina Press, 1935.

Criswell, W. A. *Fifty Years of Preaching at the Palace*. Grand Rapids: Zondervan, 1969.

Crook. Roger H. *A Tide Comes In*. Atlanta: Home Mission Board of the Southern Baptist Convention, 1967.

Current, Richard N. *Northernizing the South*. Athens: University of Georgia Press, 1983.

Dabbs, James McBride. *Haunted by God*. Richmond: John Knox Press, 1972.

Daniel, Pete. "The Transformation of the Rural South, 1930 to the Present." *Agricultural History* 55 (July 1981): 231-48.

Davenport, F. Garvin, Jr. *The Myth of Southern History: Historical Consciousness in Twentieth-Century Southern Literature.* Nashville: Vanderbilt University Press, 1970.

Dawson, Joseph Martin. *A Thousand Months to Remember.* Waco: Baylor University Press, 1964.

Dehoney, Wayne, ed. *Baptists See Black.* Waco: Word Books, 1969.

Dick, Everett. *The Dixie Frontier.* New York: Capricorn Books, 1964.

Dinnerstein, Leonard, and Mary Dale Palsson, eds. *Jews in the South.* Baton Rouge: Louisiana State University Press, 1973.

Dunbar, Anthony P. *Against the Grain: Southern Radicals and Prophets, 1929-1950.* Charlottesville: University Press of Virginia, 1981.

Earle, John R., Dean Knudsen, and Donald W. Shriver, Jr. *Spindles and Spires: A Re-Study of Religion and Social Change in Gastonia.* Atlanta: John Knox Press, 1976.

Eighmy, John Lee. *Churches in Cultural Captivity: A History of the Social Attitudes of Southern Baptists.* Knoxville: University of Tennessee Press, 1972.

Eller, Ronald D. *Miners, Millhands, and Mountaineers: Industrialization of the Appalachian South, 1880-1930.* Knoxville: University of Tennessee Press, 1972.

Encyclopedia of Religion in the South. Macon: Mercer University Press, 1984.

Encyclopedia of Southern Baptists. 4 vols. Nashville: Broadman Press, 1958-1982.

Estep, William R. "Thomas Helwys: Bold Architect of Baptist Policy on Church-State Relations." *Baptist History and Heritage* 20 (July 1985): 24-33.

Faulkner, William. *Absalom, Absalom!* New York: Vintage Books, n.d.
_____. *Go Down Moses.* New York: Vintage Books, 1973.
_____. *Intruder in the Dust.* New York: Random House, 1948.
_____. *Light in August.* New York: Vintage Books, 1972.

Fields, W. C. *Trumpets in Dixie.* Atlanta: Home Mission Board of the Southern Baptist Convention, 1967.

Fifteen Southerners, ed. *Why the South Will Survive.* Athens: University of Georgia Press, 1981.

Fitzhugh, George. *Cannibals All!* Richmond: A. Morris, 1857.
_____. *Sociology for the South.* Richmond: A. Morris, 1854.

Flynt, J. Wayne. "Dissent in Zion: Alabama Baptists and Social Issues, 1900-1914." *The Journal of Southern History* 25 (November 1969): 523-42.

_____. *Dixie's Forgotten People*. Bloomington: Indiana University Press, 1979.

Foner, Eric. *Reconstruction: America's Unifinished Revolution, 1863-1877*. New York: Harper & Row, 1988.

Fowler, Robert Booth. *A New Engagement: Evangelical Political Thought, 1966-1976*. Grand Rapids: Eerdmans, 1982.

Frady, Marshall. *Wallace*. New York: World Publishing Company, 1968.

Freidel, Frank. *F.D.R. and the South*. Baton Rouge: Louisiana State University Press, 1965.

Gaston, Paul M. *The New South Creed—A Study in Southern Mythmaking*. New York: Vintage Books, 1970.

Genovese, Eugene D. *In Red and Black: Marxian Explorations in Southern and Afro-American History*. Knoxville: University of Tennessee Press, 1984.

Gerster, Patrick, and Nicholas Cords. *Myth and Southern History*. Chicago: Rand McNally, 1974.

Gilmore, J. Herbert. *They Chose to Live: The Racial Agony of an American Church*. Grand Rapids: Eerdmans, 1972.

_____. *When Love Prevails: A Pastor Speaks to a Church in Crisis*. Grand Rapids: Eerdmans, 1971.

Grafton, Carl, and Anne Permaloff. *Big Mules & Branchheads: James E. Folsom and Political Power in Alabama*. Athens: University of Georgia Press, 1985.

Grantham, Dewey W. *The Regional Imagination: The South and Recent American History*. Nashville: Vanderbilt University Press, 1979.

Grey, J. D. "Debate, Discussion for Decision, not Division." *Baptist History and Heritage* 12 (October 1977): 231-38.

Griffin, John Howard. *Black Like Me*. New York: Signet, 1976.

Gwaltney, L. L. *Forty of the Twentieth: or, The First Forty Years of the Twentieth Century*. Birmingham: Birmingham Printing Company, 1940.

_____. *The World's Greatest Decade: The Times and the Baptists*. Birmingham: Birmingham Printing Company, 1947.

Hackney, Sheldon. "Southern Violence." *American Historical Review* 74 (February 1969): 906-25.

Hall, Jacquelyn Dowd. *Revolt Against Chivalry: Jesse Daniels Ames and the Women's Campaign Against Lynching*. New York: Columbia University Press, 1979.

Harrell, David Edwin, Jr., ed. *Varieties of Southern Evangelicalism*. Macon: Mercer University Press, 1981.

Harvard Encyclopedia of Ethnic Groups. Cambridge: Harvard University Press, 1980.

Harwell, Jack U. *Bulldozer Revolution*. Atlanta: Home Mission Board of the Southern Baptist Convention, 1967.

―――. *Teacher's Guide: Bulldozer Revolution*. Atlanta: Home Mission Board of the Southern Baptist Convention, 1967.

Hastey, Stan L. "The History and Contributions of the Baptist Joint Committee on Public Affairs." *Baptist History and Heritage* 20 (July 1985): 35-43.

―――. *Politics is my Parish*. Baton Rouge: Louisiana State University University Press, 1981.

Hays, Brooks, and John E. Steely. *The Baptist Way of Life*. Englewood Cliffs: Prentice-Hall, 1963.

Helwys, Thomas. *The Mistery of Iniquity*. Oxford: Kingsgate Press, 1935.

Hero, Alfred O. *The Southerner and World Affairs*. Baton Rouge: Louisiana State University Press, 1965.

Hill, Samuel S., Jr. *Religion and the Solid South*. Nashville: Abingdon Press, 1972.

―――. *The South and North in American Religion*. Athens: University of Georgia Press, 1980.

―――. *Southern Churches in Crisis*. New York: Holt, Rinehart and Winston, 1967.

―――, ed. *Religion in the Southern States: A Historical Study*. Macon: Mercer University Press, 1983.

Hiscox, Edward T. *The Hiscox Guide for Baptist Churches*. Valley Forge: Judson Press, 1964.

Hobson, Fred. *Tell About the South: The Southern Rage to Explain*. Baton Rouge: Louisiana State University Press, 1983.

Holman, C. Hugh. *The Immoderate Past: The Southern Writer and History*. Athens: University of Georgia Press, 1977.

Holmes, Michael S. "The Blue Eagle as Jim Crow Bird: The NRA and Georgia's Black Workers." *The Journal of Negro History* 57 (July 1972): 276-83.

Horkheimer, Max, and Theodor Adorno. *Dialectic of Enlightenment*. New York: Seabury Press, 1972.

Howard, Robert West, ed. *This is the South*. Chicago: Rand McNally, 1959.

Howe, Mark DeWolfe. *The Garden in the Wilderness: Religion and Government in American Constitutional History.* Chicago: University of Chicago Press, 1965.

Huey, Gary. *Rebel with a Cause: P. D. East, Southern Liberalism, and the Civil Rights Movement, 1953-1971.* Wilmington: Scholarly Resources, 1985.

Isaac, Rhys. *The Transformation of Virginia, 1740-1790.* Chapel Hill: University of North Carolina Press, 1982.

Jacoway, Elizabeth, and Colburn David R., eds. *Southern Businessmen and Desegregation.* Baton Rouge: Louisiana State University Press, 1972.

Johnson, Douglas, ed. *Churches and Church Membership in the United States.* Atlanta: Glenmary Research Center, 1974.

Johnson, Gerald White. *South-Watching.* Chapel Hill: University of North Carolina Press, 1983.

Jordan, Clarence. *The Substance of Faith and Other Cotton Patch Sermons.* Edited by Dallas Lee. New York: Association Press, 1972.

Kelly, Alfred H., and Winifred A. Harbison. *The American Constitution: Its Origins and Development.* New York: W. W. Norton, 1976.

Key, V. O., Jr. *Southern Politics in State and Nation.* New York: Alfred A. Knopf, 1949.

Killian, Lewis M. *White Southerners.* New York: Random House, 1970.

Kirby, Jack T. *Media-Made Dixie: The South in the American Imagination.* Baton Rouge: Louisiana State University Press, 1978.

_____. "The Transformation of Southern Plantations, 1920-1960." *Agricultural History* 57 (July 1983): 257-76.

Kousser, J. Morgan. *The Shaping of Southern Politics: Suffrage Restriction and the Formation of the One Party South, 1880-1910.* New Haven: Yale University Press, 1974.

Kurland, Philip B., ed. *Church and State: The Supreme Court and the First Amendment.* Chicago: University of Chicago Press, 1975.

LaHaye, Tim. *The Battle for the Mind.* Old Tappan: Fleming H. Revell, 1980.

_____. *The Battle for the Public Schools.* Old Tappan: Fleming H. Revell, 1983.

Lee, Dallas. *The Cotton Patch Evidence.* New York: Harper & Row, 1971.

Leland, John. *The Writings of the Late Elder John Leland, including Some Events in his Life Written by Himself.* New York: G. W. Wood, 1845.

Leonard, Bill J. "Southern Baptists and Southern Culture." *American Baptist Quarterly* 4 (June 1985): 200-213.

Lippy, Charles H. *Bibliography of Religion in the South*. Macon: Mercer University Press, 1985.

Mann, Arthur. *The One and the Many*. Chicago: University of Chicago Press, 1979.

Martin, Gerald, ed. *Great Southern Baptist Evangelistic Preaching*. Grand Rapids: Zondervan, 1969.

_____. *Great Southern Baptist Doctrinal Preaching*. Grand Rapids: Zondervan, 1969.

Masters, Victor I. *The Call of the South: A Presentation of the Home Principle in Missions, Especially as it Applies to the South*. Atlanta: Home Mission Board of the Southern Baptist Convention, 1918.

_____. "Baptists and the Christianizing of America in the New Order." *Review and Expositor* 17 (July 1920): 280-98.

Maston, T. B. *Segregation and Desegregation: A Christian Approach*. New York: Macmillan, 1959.

_____. *The Bible and Race*. Nashville: Broadman Press, 1959.

Mathews, Donald G. *Religion in the Old South*. Chicago: University of Chicago Press, 1977.

Maverick, Maury. *A Maverick American*. New York: Covici-Friede Publishers, 1937.

McBeth, Leon, "Fundamentalism in the Southern Baptist Convention in Recent Years." *Review and Expositor* 79 (Winter 1982): 85-103.

McDowell, John Patrick. *The Social Gospel in the South*. Baton Rouge: Louisiana State University Press, 1983.

McGill, Ralph. *The South and the Southerner*. Boston: Little, Brown and Company, 1963.

McKern, Sharon. *Redneck Mothers, Good Ole Girls and Other Southern Belles: A Celebration of the Women of Dixie*. New York: Viking, 1979.

McKinney, John C., and Linda Brookover Bourque. "The Changing South: National Incorporation of a Region." *American Sociological Review* 36 (June 1971): 399-412.

McKinney, John C., and Edgar T. Thompson, eds. *The South in Continuity and Change*. Durham: Duke University Press, 1965.

McLoughlin, William G. *New England Dissent, 1630-1833: The Baptists and the Separation of Church and State*. 2 vols. Cambridge: Harvard University Press, 1971.

Mencken, H. L. *A Mencken Chrestomathy*. New York: Alfred A. Knopf, 1949.

Moon, Floyce. *Teacher's Guide: A Tide Comes In*. Atlanta: Home Mission Board of the Southern Baptist Convention, 1967.

Morgan, Chester M. *Redneck Liberal: Theodore G. Bilbo and the New Deal*. Baton Rouge: Louisiana State University Press, 1985.

Morris, Willie. *Terrains of the Heart and other Essays on Home*. Oxford, Miss.: Yoknapatawpha Press, 1981.

_____. *North Towards Home*. Boston: Houghton Mifflin, 1967.

_____. *The South Today: 100 Years After Appomatax*. New York: Harper Colophon Books, 1966.

Mullins, E. Y. *Baptist Beliefs*. Philadelphia: Judson Press, 1925.

Musoke, Moses. "Mechanizing Cotton Production in the American South: The Tractor, 1915-1960." *Explorations in Economic History* 18 (October 1981): 347-75.

Newby, I. A. *The South: A History*. New York: Holt, Rinehart and Winston, 1978.

O'Brien, Michael. *The Idea of the American South, 1920-1941*. Baltimore: Johns Hopkins Press, 1979.

Odum, Howard W. *An American Epoch: Southern Portraiture in the National Picture*. Chapel Hill: University of North Carolina Press, 1930.

_____. *Southern Regions of the United States*. Chapel Hill: University of North Carolina Press, 1936.

Olson, James S. "Organized Black Leadership and Industrial Unionism: The Racial Response, 1936-1945." *Labor History* 10 (Summer 1960): 475-86.

Parker, William N. "The South in the National Economy, 1865-1970." *Southern Economic Journal* 46 (April 1980): 1019-48.

Patterson, W. Morgan, and Raymond Bryan Brown, eds. *Professor in the Pulpit: Sermons Preached in Alumni Memorial Chapel by the Faculty of The Southern Baptist Theological Seminary*. Nashville: Broadman Press, 1963.

Phillips, Ulrich B. "The Central Theme of Southern History." *American Historical Review* 35 (1928): 30-43.

Pope, Liston. *Millhands and Preachers: A Study of Gastonia*. New Haven: Yale University Press, 1942.

Prenshaw, Peggy W., and Jesse O. McKee, eds. *Sense of Place: Mississippi*. Jackson: University Press of Mississippi, 1979.

Raines, Howell. *My Soul is Rested: Movement Days in the Deep South Remembered*. New York: G. P. Putnam's Sons, 1977.

Reed, John Shelton. *The Enduring South: Subcultural Persistence in Mass Society*. Chapel Hill: University of North Carolina Press, 1974.

_____. *Southerners: The Social Psychology of Sectionalism*. Chapel Hill: University of North Carolina Press, 1983.

Rigdon, Doris, and Raymond Rigdon. *Teacher's Guide: Trumpets in Dixie*. Atlanta: Home Mission Board of the Southern Baptist Convention, 1967.

Roebuck, Julian B., Mark and Hickson III. *The Southern Redneck: A Phenomenological Class Study*. New York: Praeger, 1982.

Roland, Charles P. "The Ever-Vanishing South." *Journal of Southern History* 48 (February 1982): 3-20.

_____. *The Improbable Era: The South Since World War II*. Lexington: University Press of Kentucky, 1975.

Rubin, Louis D., Jr. *William Elliott Shoots a Bear: Essays on the Southern Literary Imagination*. Baton Rouge: Louisiana State University Press, 1975.

_____. *The American South*. Baton Rouge: Louisiana State University Press, 1980.

_____. *A Bibliographical Guide to the Study of Southern Literature*. Baton Rouge: Louisiana State University Press, 1969.

Rubin, Louis D., and James J. Kilpatrick, eds. *The Lasting South*. Chicago: Henry Regnery Co., 1957.

Rymph, Raymond C., and Jeffrey K. Hadden. "The Persistence of Regionalism in Racial Attitudes of Methodist Clergy." *Social Forces* 49 (September 1970): 41-50.

Sale, Kirkpatrick. *Power Shift*. New York: Vintage Books, 1975.

Scott, Anne Firor. *The Southern Lady: From Pedestal to Politics, 1830-1930*. Chicago: University of Chicago Press, 1970.

Sellers, James L. "The Economic Incidence of the Civil War in the South." *Mississippi Valley Historical Review* 14 (1927-28): 183-89.

Shurden, Walter B. *Not a Silent People: Controversies That Have Shaped Southern Baptists*. Nashville: Broadman Press, 1972.

Singal, Daniel Joseph. *The War Within: From Victorian to Modernist Thought in the South, 1919-1945*. Chapel Hill: University of North Carolina Press, 1982.

Skaggs, William Henry. *The Southern Oligarchy: An Appeal in Behalf of the Silent Masses of Our Country Against the Despotic Rule of the Few*. New York: Devin-Adair, 1924.

Smith, Lillian. *Killers of the Dream*. New York: Norton, 1949.

_____. *Strange Fruit*. New York: Reynal & Hitchcock, 1944.

Smylie, James H. "The Roman Catholic Church, the State, and Al Smith." *Church History* 29 (September 1960): 321-43.

Snyder, Robert E. *Cotton Crisis*. Chapel Hill: University of North Carolina Press, 1984.

Southern Commission on the Study of Lynching. *Lynchings and What They Mean*. Atlanta, The Commission, n.d.

The Southern Tradition at Bay: A History of Postbellum Thought. New Rochelle: Arlington House, 1968.

Spain, Rufus B. *At Ease in Zion: Social History of Southern Baptists, 1865-1900*. Nashville: Vanderbilt University Press, 1967.

Stokes, Anson Phelps, and Pfeffer, Leo. *Church and State in the United States*. Rev. ed. New York: Harper & Row, 1964.

Styron, William. *Sophie's Choice*. New York: Bantam Books, 1980.

Sullivan, Clayton. *Called to Preach, Condemned to Survive: The Education of Clayton Sullivan*. Macon: Mercer University Press, 1985.

Thomas, Norman C. *Education in National Politics*. New York: David McKay Company, 1975.

Thompson, James J., Jr. *Tried as By Fire: Southern Baptists and the Religious Controversies of the 1920's*. Macon: Mercer University Press, 1982.

Tindall, George B. *The Emergence of the New South: 1913-1946*. Baton Rouge: Louisiana State University Press, 1967.

_____. *The Ethnic Southerners*. Baton Rouge: Louisiana State University Press, 1976.

Twelve Southerners. *I'll Take My Stand: The South and the Agrarian Tradition*. Gloucester, Mass.: Peter Smith, [1930] 1976.

United States Department of Commerce, Bureau of the Census. *Statistical Abstract of the United States, 1938*. Washington, D.C.: Government Printing Office, 1938.

Vance, Rupert. *Regionalism and the South*. Chapel Hill: University of North Carolina Press, 1982.

_____. "Beyond the Fleshpots: The Coming Culture Crisis in the South." *Virginia Quarterly Review* 41 (Spring 1965): 222.

Vandiver, Frank E. *The Idea of the South: Pursuit of a Central Theme*. Chicago: University of Chicago Press, 1964.

Wamble, G. Hugh. "Baptist Contributions to Separation of Church and State." *Baptist History and Heritage* 20 (July 1985): 3-13.

Watson, Richard L., Jr., "The Defeat of Judge Parker: A Study in Pressure Groups and Politics." *Mississippi Valley Historical Review* 50 (1963-1964): 213-34.

Whisnant, David E. *All That is Native and Fine*. Chapel Hill: University of North Carolina Press, 1983.

White, W. R. *Baptist Distinctives*. Nashville: Sunday School Board, 1946.

White, Walter F. *Rope and Faggot: A Biography of Judge Lynch*. New York: Alfred A. Knopf, 1929.

Woodward, C. Vann. *Origins of the New South, 1877-1913*. Baton Rouge: Louisiana State University Press, 1951.

_____. *The Burden of Southern History*. Baton Rouge: Louisiana State University Press, 1960.

_____. *The Strange Career of Jim Crow*. 3rd rev. ed. New York: Oxford University Press, 1974.

_____. *Thinking Back: The Perils of Writing History*. Baton Rouge: Louisiana State University Press, 1986.

Index

Abolitionists, 83
Abortion, 71-73
Absalom, Absalom! (Faulkner), 46, 48
Adorno, Theodor, 2
Agriculture, 35
Ahlstrom, Sydney, ix
Alabama Baptist, 91, 93
Alabama Baptist Convention, 88
Alcohol, 70
All the King's Men (Warren), 50
America, 110
America, Christianizing, 16
American Baptist Bill of Rights, 101, 102
American Council of Education, 105
American Revolution, 13
Amos, 64
Andrews, George, 110-111
Anti-Catholicism, 103. *See also* Roman
  Catholics
Anticolonialism, 95
Apartheid, 79
Association of Southern Women for the
  Prevention of Lynching, 38
Authority, 9

Babbitt, Irving, 44
Baggett, Dr. Hudson, 66
Baptism, 18, 119n
Baptist colleges, 106, 107
Baptist Joint Committee on Public Affairs,
  61, 102, 111, 115
Baptists, 3, 7
  beliefs of, 17-21
  British, 98
  and colonies, 11, 13
  equality of, 14
  and evangelism, 11
  and individual congregation, 19

as ministers, 12-13
and politics, 114
Primitive, 3
and South, 16
split over slavery, 15
Two-seed-in-the-spirit, 3
See also Southern Baptist Convention;
  Southern Baptists
Barton, Arthur, 84
Becker Amendment, 111, 113
Beliefs, 17-21, 87
Bellows, Barbara L., 122n
Benjamin, John C., 122n
Bennet, William, 103
Bible, inerrancy of, 73
  reading, 109, 111
  and slavery, 83
Bilbo, Theodore, 39, 128n
Birmingham, Alabama, 29-30, 39, 56, 90
Black Like Me (Griffin), 40
Black power movement, 77
Blacks, 25-26
  as culturally inferior, 83
  in schools, 110
  versus whites, 76
  voting patterns of, 38
  See also Black power movement; Civil
  Rights
Blount, Roy, 36
Bond, Julian, 66
Boyd, Blanche McCrary, 36
Breckinridge, Judah P., 122n
Brewer, Albert, 39
Briand-Kellogg Pact, 59
Brown v. Board of Education, 82
Bulldozer Revolution, 90
Bunyan, John, 88
Butler, James, 39-40

Chicago Studies in the History of American Religion

Editors

JERALD C. BRAUER & MARTIN E. MARTY

(continued, over)